# Virtual Educational Therapy

*Virtual Educational Therapy* presents a board-certified educational therapist's year-long case study of clinical supports and advocacy for a student with learning disabilities who is attending school remotely during the COVID-19 pandemic. With online and blended learning, now the norm in K–12 education, educational therapists need new models of intervention, treatment, and relationship-building for their child-age clients. This book offers detailed single-case research focused on a middle-school student who is learning virtually while challenged with ADHD as well as visual and verbal memory issues, but who is nonetheless found ineligible for special education services. Across eight chapters, author and renowned educational therapist Marion E. Marshall describes the neuropsychological principles, research-based techniques, personal interactions, clinical approaches, and advocacy efforts that led to a vulnerable student's significant gains in academic skills and outcomes.

**Marion E. Marshall**, MS, BCET, FAET, is Emerita Professor, former Director of the Educational Therapy Program, and Founding Faculty Member in the Center for Excellence in Teaching and Learning at Holy Names University, USA. A Board-Certified Educational Therapist, Credentialed Special Educator, and Independent School Learning Specialist, she was Clinical Director of the Raskob Day School and Learning Institute in Oakland, California.

# Virtual Educational Therapy
A Case Study of Clinical Supports and Advocacy

Marion E. Marshall

Routledge
Taylor & Francis Group
NEW YORK AND LONDON

First published 2023
by Routledge
605 Third Avenue, New York, NY 10158

and by Routledge
4 Park Square, Milton Park, Abingdon, Oxon, OX14 4RN

*Routledge is an imprint of the Taylor & Francis Group, an informa business*

© 2023 Marion E. Marshall

The right of Marion E. Marshall to be identified as author of this work has been asserted in accordance with sections 77 and 78 of the Copyright, Designs and Patents Act 1988.

All rights reserved. No part of this book may be reprinted or reproduced or utilised in any form or by any electronic, mechanical, or other means, now known or hereafter invented, including photocopying and recording, or in any information storage or retrieval system, without permission in writing from the publishers.

*Trademark notice*: Product or corporate names may be trademarks or registered trademarks, and are used only for identification and explanation without intent to infringe.

*Library of Congress Cataloging-in-Publication Data*
A catalog record for this book has been requested

ISBN: 978-1-032-25733-4 (hbk)
ISBN: 978-1-032-32458-6 (pbk)
ISBN: 978-1-003-28474-1 (ebk)

DOI: 10.4324/9781003284741

Typeset in Times New Roman
by Apex CoVantage, LLC

**My heartfelt thank you**

**to Geoff Underwood** for always encouraging me to be my best, who read over and over again, and was still enthusiastic about the book.

**to Risa Graff, BCET,** whose suggestions greatly enhanced this work.

**to Dorothy Ungerleider,** who has inspired us all.

**to "Maya,"** who has a sky full of gold stars in her future.

# Contents

*List of figures and tables* x
*Preface: Regarding the Case Study Methodology* xi

**1 The Case of Maya – Background** 1
*Exploratory Educational Therapy Session 2*
*The Writing Interview 3*
*"Stay Put" Invoked 3*
*Key Findings From the Neuropsychology Report 4*
  *Implications for Educational Therapy 5*
*Attention and Executive Functioning 6*
  *Implications for Educational Therapy 6*
*Memory and Learning 6*
  *Implications for Educational Therapy 7*
  *Social and Emotional Status 7*
    *Implications for Educational Therapy 8*
*Why Do Students Struggle to Write? 8*
*A Process Approach to Educational Therapy 9*
*Summary 9*

**2 Engagement and Learning** 11
*Engagement, Motivation, and Effort 11*
*Maya's Interests 12*
*Organizing Her Ideas in Writing – The Four Square Approach 13*
*Each New Session 14*
*Creating a Vocabulary Ladder 15*

*Gold Stars 15*
*Using the Four Square Method 15*
*IEP Meeting for the IEE Process 17*
*Missing Fundamentals 18*
*Summary 20*

**3 Writing Beyond Her Direct Experience**   23
*Disneyland Is Closed Due to COVID-19 23*
*Reading From Winnie the Pooh and Visualization 24*
*Establishing the Learning Purpose 25*
*Reading and Writing from ReadWorks Articles 26*
*When Not Medicated 27*
*Science Research Paper 27*
*IEP Meeting Attended by Maya's Family's Lawyer 28*
*Summary 30*

**4 More Sustained Reading and Writing**   32
*Establishing New IEP Goals 32*
*Sustained Reading and Writing 33*
*Cinderella to Yeh-Shen 33*
*Chinye and Aschenputtel 35*
*Writing Using Transition Words 35*
*Summary 36*

**5 Applying Other Strategies**   38
*Notetaking to Improve Writing 38*
*School Required Reading 39*
*They Don't Care 40*
*Tomtar 41*
*Creative Writing 42*
*Summary 44*

**6 Superheroes and Greek Gods and Goddesses**   45
*Greek Gods and Goddesses 46*
*Integrating Mechanics While Writing 48*
*Creating Character Studies 48*
*Using Mad Libs 50*
*More Creative Writing 50*
*Self-directed Learning 51*

*Writing a Persuasive Essay: Crystals* 52
*Essay Preparation* 53
*Saliency Determination* 54
*Summary* 56

## 7 The Final Three Months     57
*Trial Preparation* 57
*Further Shocking Discoveries* 58
*Arbitration Hearing* 60
   *Regarding Special Education Law Challenges* 60
   *WIAT III Assessment by the District* 61
*Why Had Maya Scored So Well?* 63
*One Year Later – Neuropsychology Reassessment* 64
*Summer Work – Executive Functioning* 65
*Examining Her Strengths* 66
*Summer Work – Reading Novels* 67
*Reading –* Hello, Universe *68*
*Making Predictions* 69
*Pacing* 70
*Mark and Defend* 71
*Reading –* When You Trap a Tiger *73*
*Her Reading Expands* 73
*IEP Meeting to Begin 8th Grade* 75
*Summary* 75

## 8 The Case of Maya: Summary     77
*Summary* 81

*Index*     82

# Figures and Tables

**Figures**

| | | |
|---|---|---:|
| 2.1 | Her Writing Process | 16 |
| 2.2 | Example of Four Square Graphic Organizer Using Engagement Concepts | 19 |
| 7.1 | Kaori – Character Study | 72 |

**Tables**

| | | |
|---|---|---:|
| 7.1 | WIAT III Results | 62 |

# Preface: Regarding the Case Study Methodology

A case study is a research approach that is used to generate an in-depth, multifaceted understanding of a complex issue in its real-life context. It is both time- and space-bound and is useful to explore, describe, and explain phenomena. It is an established research design that is used extensively in a wide variety of disciplines, particularly in the social sciences, including education. Many master's programs employ the case study methodology as the basis for the culminating project. The Association of Educational Therapists (AET) requires a case study as one of the requisites for earning Board Certification https://aetonline.org/index.php/members-center/become-board-certified (Association of Educational Therapists, 2022). The case study methodology is especially relevant to advancing "younger disciplines" such as educational therapy. Many do not understand the training and difference in approaches between an Educational Therapist (ET) and a tutor, so publishing case studies is crucial.

A search of the literature was conducted using EBSCO, a university research database. Eleven journal articles published between 1982 and 2020 were found. The most recent was a case study of a math learning disability; it was published in the *Elsevier Journal of Mathematical Behavior* (Lewis, K. E. 2020). There are case studies included as a chapter in books published by Routledge, *The Clinical Practice of Educational Therapy: A Teaching Model* (2010) and *Best Practices in Educational Therapy* (2019). There are two case studies of adults in books by Dorothy Ungerleider, the founding president of AET: *Educational Therapy in Action: Behind and Beyond the Office Door* (2011) and *Reading, Writing, and Rage* (1985). These works are seminal and read by nearly every educational therapist, either while in training or as a touchstone for comparison to their own work. Clearly, there is a need for additional publications, especially detailing work conducted virtually.

Researchers name the sources of evidence in case studies as interviews, documentation, archival records, physical artifacts, and direct observations of the student working. This case study employs all of these sources of evidence.

Not every session, technique, or activity employed is chronicled in this case study. Instead, the sessions where important issues, hypotheses, and pivotal moments occurred are detailed and discussed.

## References

Association of Educational Therapists. (2022, January 10). *Becoming board certified.* https://aetonline.org/index.php/members-center/become-board-certified

EBSCO Research Databases. www.ebsco.com/products/research-databases/academic-search-ultimate

Ficksman, M., & Adelizzi, J. U. (2010). *The clinical practice of educational therapy: A teaching model.* Routledge.

Kaganoff, A. P. (2019). *Best practices in educational therapy.* Routledge.

Lewis, K. E. (2020). Integer number sense and notation: A case study of a student with a mathematics learning disability. www.sciencedirect.com/science/article/abs/pii/S0732312320300614

Ungerleider, D. F. (1985). *Reading writing and rage: The terrible price paid by victims of school failure.* RWR Press.

Ungerleider, D. F. (2011). *Educational therapy in action: Behind and beyond the office door.* Routledge.

## Resources

Bartlett, L., & Vavrus, F. (2017). *Rethinking case study research.* Routledge.

Baskarada, S. (2014, October 19). Qualitative case study guidelines. *The Qualitative Report, 19*(40), 1–25. SSRN 2559424.

Baxter, P., & Jack, S. (2008). Qualitative case study methodology: Study design and implementation for novice researchers. *The Qualitative Report, 13*(4), 544–559.

Eisenhardt, K. M. (1989). Building theories from case study research. *The Academy of Management Review, 14*(4), 532–550. doi:10.2307/258557. JSTOR 258557

George, A. L., & Bennett, A. (2005). *Case studies and theory development in the social sciences.* MIT Press. ISBN 0-262-57222-2.

Gerring, J. (2008). *Case study research.* Cambridge University Press. ISBN 978-0-521-67656-4.

Mills, A. J., Durepos, G., & Wiebe, E. (Eds.). (2010). *Encyclopedia of case study research.* SAGE Publications. ISBN 978-1-4129-5670-3.

Ragin, C. C., & Becker, H. S. (Eds.). (1992). *What is a case? Exploring the foundations of social inquiry.* Cambridge University Press. ISBN 0-521-42188-8.

Scholz, R. W., & Tietje, O. (2002). *Embedded case study methods. Integrating quantitative and qualitative knowledge.* SAGE Publications. ISBN 0-7619-1946-5.

Thomas, G. (2011). *How to do your case study: A guide for students and researchers.* SAGE Publications.

# 1 The Case of Maya – Background

"Wait! Wait! I have strengths? Can I tell them to my mother?"

At times I felt as though I had three clients with competing needs – Maya, who had very limited reading and writing skills, her parents, who had come to believe that she was quite impaired, and the recalcitrant school district which had exited her from special education services.

This single-client case study follows "Maya", a 13-year-old, for the 12 months of her 7th-grade year and the following summer during COVID-19. She was taught virtually at her public school for the entire year during the COVID pandemic. Maya was seen by this educational therapist virtually, as well. She had a long history of attention-deficit/hyperactivity disorder (ADHD), dysgraphia, and a Specific Learning Disability (a written language disorder), and got qualified for special education services in the 3rd grade.

Maya lived with her father (a technology researcher), her mother (a homemaker), and her older brother of 17. She lived in a community outside of the geographical area where the researcher normally saw clients. Her school district was ranked in the top 10% out of the 438 school districts in California. The annual median household income was $160,000. Less than 5% of the students received free or reduced lunches. Eighty percent of the household listed their ethnicity as either Asian or White (www.niche.com/k12/d/xxxx-unified-school-district-ca/students/).

The parents had never heard of educational therapy but immediately acted on the recommendation to have one to work with Maya, following her recent neuropsychological assessment. They began interviewing and subsequently hired this educational therapist. As a part of that initial conversation with the parents, I was asked if I could work with a student having a written language disorder. I explained that I had worked successfully with many students who had writing issues and discussed some of the techniques I used. The parents asked if I would attend IEP meetings. I explained that I would and hoped

DOI: 10.4324/9781003284741-1

to work in collaboration with the school team. Her father replied, "That ship has sailed" and added they were disputing the school district's decision (at the triennial review) that Maya had met all of her IEP goals and had passing grades so was no longer qualified to receive special education services.

In the initial intake conversation with her mother, she shared that Maya was cooperative and "easy to engage if she was interested in the topic or activity" and that school "thought her very ADHD" but the family "doesn't see it so much. . . . We see her as funny and are used to her randomness. . . . Her interests are just a bit offbeat" and "She is very likable. . . . She has very deep and loyal friendships with the same group of kids."

## Exploratory Educational Therapy Session

The complementary exploratory session was designed to determine several things. Could Maya engage via Zoom? How long could she focus? Did she have a writing process? Was there an underlying expressive language issue? What was her attitude toward writing? Was there any aspect of writing she enjoyed? As she had never worked with an outside support provider before, what was her attitude? Could she be a willing partner? Could I deliver effective educational therapy given that I was so accustomed to closely observing and attuning myself to the student's nonverbal behaviors, which would be harder to notice on a computer screen?

In the exploratory session, I found Maya sitting on her bed, which surprised me but I did not challenge her. I employed "the silent conversation" technique where "get-to-know-you" questions are asked but answered silently in writing. In this case of virtual communication, we used whiteboards. I asked, "Do you have any pets?"

She wrote, "7."

I wrote back, "What kind of pets?"

Maya answered, "2 dogs 2 fish 3 cats"

I prompted, "Now ask me a question" (by writing).

She responded readily with, "do you have any pets" (no capital or ending punctuation).

We continued the "silent conversation" for a few more minutes and she was able to generate follow-up questions for me. My subsequent notes state that her spelling was good; longer sentences had no beginning capitalization or ending punctuation. Her responses were short but germane and she printed using overly large letter formation. I also noted she hummed or sang quietly. "What are you singing, Maya?"

"Nothing. Just a song. I sing to myself a lot."

"Would I know the song?"

"No, it's just something I made up; it doesn't have any words."

## The Writing Interview

I verbally asked Maya many of the questions on *The Writing Interview* in Educational Care: A System for Understanding and Helping Children with Learning Problems at Home and in School *Educational Care* (2002). She agreed with three of the five statements having to do with graphomotor function such as "Kids sometimes complain that their hand gets very tired when they have to write a lot" and "Some people can print much better than they can use cursive" to which she added, "I NEVER use cursive! I only print."

She endorsed none of the states regarding difficulties with expressive language and only one of the four statements about ideation (coming up with ideas), "Some students find it very hard to think up topics or decide what they want to write about." Maya agreed that "[s]ometimes it was hard to think of things to write about" and "It can be very difficult to know what to include in a report." She agreed with two out of the five items involving memory. "It is confusing to remember so many things at once (like spelling, punctuation, vocabulary, etc.) while writing."

"It's IMPOSSIBLE!" she stated. Lastly, Maya endorsed three statements regarding organization when writing. She found it hard to get started, didn't think much in advance about what she was going to write or how to write it, and agreed that it was hard to know how long it would take to write a report. Actually, she commented that she did know how long a report would take – TOO LONG! She "hated peer-editing because others could see her work" and judge it. When asked what was most difficult about writing, Maya stated, "It's all hard." When asked what does a student need to be good at to write well, she responded optimistically, "All kids can get better at writing!"

Maya's mother called me later to ask if I was willing to take her daughter as a client. "She liked you! She cooperated! She said she was willing to work with you for the two sessions a week you require." Later, she told me she had been sitting outside Maya's door (unbeknown to Maya or me). She thought it was very clever to get some writing samples without the student realizing it.

## "Stay Put" Invoked

Unknown to this educational therapist and despite obvious learning challenges, Maya had been determined to be ineligible for special education services at the Individualized Education Program, IEP, meeting just prior to the educational therapist beginning to work with her. Nor was this educational therapist aware, at the outset, of the results of the recent neuropsychology assessment, only that one had been conducted recently. Therefore, her tenuous educational status added a sense of urgency to the support needed while her parents mounted a formal appeal via an Independent Educational Evaluation, IEE.

Parents who disagree with the results of their child's evaluation have the right to obtain an evaluation conducted by a qualified examiner who is not employed by the public school district, usually at their own expense. It was puzzling to understand why her district would be so adamant about discontinuing services in the face of her parents' challenge. Why would a district risk a lawsuit over one student remaining in an already-existing resource specialist class?

Maya had been medicated for ADHD on and off during her 3rd–6th-grade years. She was not medicated when assessed by a prominent developmental neuropsychologist as documentation for the IEE just prior to the commencement of the educational therapist's work with Maya. In fact, when the neuropsychologist gave her initial oral report to Maya's parents, she stressed the need for Maya to begin working with an experienced educational therapist while the parents advocated for continued resource specialist support in her current school placement. A "stay put" order was invoked by her parents. According to understood.org, "The 'stay put' provision is one of the most important legal rights in special education law and applies when a parent or guardian disputes a change the school wants to make to a child's IEP." The law requires maintenance of "the status quo" for the student while the dispute is pending. The courts have recognized that in creating the "stay put" provision, Congress meant to prevent districts from having the power to unilaterally change a child's placement. This aligns with the section of the *Individuals with Disabilities Education Act*'s (IDEA) emphasis on parent participation in the educational decisions for their children. See 20 U.S.C. §1412(a)(5)(A); 34 C.F.R. §§300.550(b)(1) & (2).

As a result of invoking this right, Maya would continue to receive resource specialist services for one (virtual) period per day, while working with this educational therapist. Her parents had hired a special education advocate to help negotiate with the district. Upon learning this, I was relieved thinking that the advocate would do the "heavy lifting" and I could focus solely on remediation.

Later, I found this was not the case and my role would soon include the role of advocate with her school.

## Key Findings From the Neuropsychology Report

The key findings of the Neuropsychology Report are detailed here along with the implications for the educational therapist in supporting Maya. The Neuropsychologist conducted interviews, records review, evaluation, and school observation (via Zoom) between July and September 2020. Two three-hour assessments were held using the following instruments:

The Wechsler Intelligence Scale for Children – V, Gray Oral Reading Test – V, Test of Written Language-4 (TOWL-4), Behavior Rating Inventory of Executive Function – 2nd Edition Parent Self-reports, Projective Drawings, the Rey-Osterrieth Complex Figure, Behavior Assessment System for Children – 3, Parent and Self Forms, Test of Variables of Attention, Children and Adolescent Memory Profile, Kaufman Test of Educational Achievement – 3, and stories from the Children's Memory Scale, and Sentenced Completion.

According to the report, Maya had "age-expected normal intelligence" and "a significant case of Attention Deficit Hyperactivity Disorder." She met the criteria for the combined type as she "had high levels of restlessness and distractibility." She struggled to such a significant degree that a specific learning disability (DSM-5) diagnosis code was applied "due to a significant discrepancy between her intelligence and her independent written output." Difficulties with written expression such as punctuation errors, organization, and restricted output were all noted.

Although Maya "could spell single words at an expected level, she struggled greatly when asked to compose a paragraph." "If translated, her writing score into a grade equivalence, it is as low as the 2nd grade." While her performance "indicated some nice ideas, there was no punctuation, run-on sentences, and little elaboration." When she was presented with specific written rules she had to follow: start every sentence with a capital; remember punctuation; organize the story into beginning, middle, and end; and organize it into paragraphs, her writing improved "a bit." A day later, when these rules were no longer visible, Maya was given a parallel story prompt on the TOWL-4. Her writing no longer reflected these reminders. "These are not internalized by her [written] text." (TOWL-4 Contextual Conventions Scaled Score 7; Story Composition Scaled Score 6; Total called Scaled Score 79 = 8th percentile rank.)

Her reading skills followed a similar pattern in that she could "read words at grade level" and "pull out factual information from a text"; she struggled with reading comprehension when needing to "extract information that is not explicitly stated, predict, or draw conclusions."

## *Implications for Educational Therapy*

Maya's good intellect was masked by her ADHD, her inattentiveness, and her impulsivity. Reading comprehension and writing both require significant working memory, which she lacked. She spelled single words well and read single words accurately. These skills are helpful in the earlier grades and primarily rely on visual memory skills. Reading and writing, in 3rd grade and beyond, require sustained attention, organization, and an *integration* of skills. Writing mechanics would need to be retaught. Strategies which teach organization would be necessary. Visual prompts might be helpful tools.

## Attention and Executive Functioning

Maya's self-rating indicated that she had attention problems at the "clinical chronically significant range." She recognized being told often to pay attention and stated that she had "difficulty paying attention to the teacher." She knew that she was "easily distracted, had difficulty concentrating, and that she forgets what she was supposed to do." Both Maya and her parents reported significant difficulties with keeping impulses at bay while keeping information in mind.

Maya was "notably distracted and restless, yet always compliant" during the assessment. On a direct attention test where the student sits for 20 minutes and performs a computer-based task of pressing a button when an icon appears in the screen (the TOVA), Maya sat and looked at the screen, yet the results indicated "very significant attentional deficits." Her omission errors were very significant. "Her score (-6.85) was a striking finding because it was not evident while observing Maya doing the test, as she smiled and kept at it." The BASC-3 (Parent Rating) scores for Hyperactivity and Attention Problems were at "the significant level." On the BASC-3 (Child Self-Rating), Maya's scores were "at the significant level" for Interpersonal Relations, Self-Esteem, Self-Reliance, and at the Elevated Level: Attitude Towards School, Social Stress, Anxiety, Depression, Attention Problems, and Hyperactivity.

### *Implications for Educational Therapy*

Maya knew she struggled with focusing and sustaining her attention. She could appear attentive when she was actually *internally focusing* elsewhere. Missing her teacher's directions caused her anxiety. The one-to-one nature of educational therapy might ameliorate some of her distractibility, but how would she cope with working via Zoom? Teaching, notetaking, and reading comprehension strategies could help her focus and retain information. Strategies which taught her how to determine saliency would be important. Techniques which fostered engagement would be essential.

## Memory and Learning

Memory testing was also conducted by the neuropsychologist. "This is deemed an important area to assess given that it reveals how the student takes in and learns new information." Maya's results were "quite concerning." On a standard battery (ChAMP), Maya's overall index score was at the 1st percentile. She had great difficulty "learning both verbally presented and visually presented information." With repetition, she improved on both subtests. However, when asked to recall information half an hour later, her recall was "quite poor." The neuropsychologist's report stated, "she can learn in the moment, but easily."

When two stories (CMS) were read aloud to Maya and she was asked to retell them immediately and after a half-hour delay, her rendition of the story "contained only approximately 10% of the material" and she missed the essential point. After half an hour, her recall "was even weaker, with approximately only 5%" remembered.

Her ability to copy the design [on the Rey-Osterrieth Complex Figure] was "adequate" at the 16th percentile", but when the design was removed and she was asked to draw it again, her performance was "exceedingly poor – dropping down to the 1st percentile."

## *Implications for Educational Therapy*

According to the report, Maya's recall was exceedingly limited. However, one cannot remember what was not attended to in the first place. "Learning" that is superficial, not understood well, or not valued degrades quickly. Making meaning for Maya would be important. Verifying her understanding of any "new learning" would be critical. Repeated practice with new concepts would be crucial and would need to be delivered incrementally. The pace of teaching new skills would need to be judged carefully and Maya's retention verified regularly.

## *Social and Emotional Status*

Maya reported "anxiety, social stress, and test anxiety." She reported that she often "worries, feels nervous, and feels sad." In contrast, her parents described Maya as having a "happy personality, being friendly, able to adapt easily to change, and follow rules."

Her learning disabilities were described as "moderate to severe" by the neuropsychologist and she stated that "the SLD affected multiple domains and intensive services and specialized teaching were needed for several years." The report also stated that "she will not become proficient unless she has intensive and specialized teaching on an ongoing basis." The neuropsychologist's report also acknowledged that Maya's multiple disabilities could appear "invisible in the company of adults." She would look directly at an adult so that it "seemed that she is listening and paying attention. However, she was not."

*Implications for Educational Therapy*

Learning and retaining new information was challenging for Maya. It was no wonder that her self-esteem was affected. Yes, she seemed to be trying to please the adults around her. I had noted that she seemed self-aware, especially about what she knew how to do and when she was unclear about something. If she perceived her difficulties as clearly as they seemed, this would cause a great deal of distress. Monitoring her emotional state would be critical.

In summary, according to the neuropsychologist's report, Maya met special education eligibility for both "Specific Learning Disability as well as Other Health Impaired (in light of ADHD)." "Both her writing challenges as well as other academic difficulties in addition to her ADHD have an impact on her education." Her difficulties in retaining new information were "significant." Her "sinking self-esteem and increasing distress around her academic struggles" were "noteworthy."

The implications of these assessment results seemed quite bleak. In all honesty, had I known the full extent of this evaluation, I might not have accepted Maya as a client fearing the seemingly nearly impossible task of helping Maya make a significant improvement in her writing skills. Yet, I remained cautiously optimistic since she had responded well and with adequate attention for the 30 minutes of the exploratory session. I noted that Maya was very outspoken and candid in her views regarding her schooling and her own experiences of learning. This frankness was refreshing in a young teen and might assist greatly in the remediation process. This level of self-awareness seemed unusual, especially with a new client.

With the neuropsychologist's report in mind, I reflected on why students struggle with writing.

## Why Do Students Struggle to Write?

First, written language is based on one's inner language. Students who have limited expressive language skills usually struggle to write. Students who are learning English may not have the necessary English vocabulary to write easily. Writing also depends upon receptive language, background knowledge, and vocabulary. It requires ideation, spelling, syntax, grammar, writing mechanics, orthographic knowledge, and handwriting. Written language is a challenge for many students since it requires a synthesis of all these skills. This need for synthesis creates a higher demand for working memory as compared to any other academic skill. Focal maintenance when writing requires a high degree of attention and executive functioning skills (Marshall, 2020).

Maya struggled with many critical skills necessary to write easily: attention, sustaining her focus, understanding and employing writing mechanics, and the ability to use a pencil as an efficient tool. However, her conversational expressive language appeared adequate, which seemed hopeful.

Later, it seemed that her background knowledge was very limited; if she had not seen the movie, she did not know much about the topic; her vocabulary was "movie-centric" too. She had a vague understanding of a word based on how the actor or actress said or portrayed the word's meaning in a movie scene.

"Maya, do you know what the word "sarcasm" means?

"I know what that word means. I just can't explain it."

"Try."

"Well, in the Marvel movie, The Eternals, Phastos says, 'You know what never saved the planet? Your sarcasm.' So, it's like a joke."

Nor did she recall much about the topics previously studied – even as recently as the year prior.

"I think we studied the Greek and Roman gods and goddesses last year, but I don't remember much about it." Later, when reading about Persephone in an Educational Therapy session, she exclaimed, "Hey! This seems kinda familiar! Wait! Wait! I did a report about her last year."

This lack of recall echoed what the neuropsychologist's report had stated.

## A Process Approach to Educational Therapy

As an Educational Therapist, I use a "process approach" in my work. My decision-making process is based on an intuitive understanding of a client's needs, any formal available assessment results (mine or others'), and on 40 years of experience. There is the very valuable informal data collection that involves observation, taking notes, and reflecting on what that recently gleaned information might mean. I use the term "process notes" to denote all of that collected input, session data, and reflective and hypothesis questioning. I keep track of my discoveries and any questions that arise in order to refine my understanding of the case. In the chapter summaries of this book, I have endeavored to illustrate some of my thought processes/clinical thinking.

## Summary

To date, I learned several things about Maya and answered some of my initial questions about her ability to engage with me via Zoom and her general level of attention and cooperation. I had learned that Maya was forthright in discussing her strengths and weaknesses. She appeared to know herself well. I felt a cautious optimism about our work together and wondered about her vocabulary, background knowledge, and current writing skills. I had read the neuropsychologist's assessment report with interest and a sense of timidity. This chapter describes the assessment report's implications for this educational therapist's intervention plan. The educational therapist suspected that Maya's views about what she would and would not do were often accepted by her mother and that Maya's mother was quite protective of her daughter.

## References

Individuals with Disabilities Education Act "Stay Put" retrieved from: 20 U.S.C. §1412(a)(5)(A); 34 C.F.R. §§300.550(b)(1) & (2).

Levine, M. (1994). *Educational Care: A System for Understanding and Helping Children with Learning Problems at Home and in School.* Educators Publishing Service, Inc. ISBN 0838819877.

Marshall, M. E. (2020). *Assessment in educational therapy.* Routledge.

*Niche.com.* www.niche.com/k12/d/xxxx -unified-school-district-ca/students/

# 2 Engagement and Learning

A key to helping Maya focus in our sessions, master new material, and retain new learning would be creating a high degree of engagement. What is engagement?

One of the most outstanding differences in educating students during the COVID pandemic was the lack of engagement created by distance learning. In education, engagement refers to the degree of attention, curiosity, interest, and passion that students show when they are learning or being taught (www.edglossary.org/student-engagement/ Feb 2016).

This extends to a student's internal motivation to learn. As an educational therapist, I have always valued the freedom to "customize" and tailor the content to engage the learner. Whereas, a tutor will reteach or pre-teach school-determined curricula. Research has validated the connections between "noncognitive factors" such as motivation, interest, curiosity, responsibility, determination, perseverance, attitude, work habits, self-regulation, and learning especially in the online space (Martin, F. & Bolliger, D. U. 2018). So, using a student's interest is not merely an educational therapist's tool, it is an important means of fostering learning.

## Engagement, Motivation, and Effort

Additional research has found that student engagement enhances student motivation to learn and reduces the sense of isolation (Banna et al., 2015). Many students felt disconnected in the online learning environment. Maya felt it keenly. She felt cut off from her teachers and her close friends. When asked if she could ask her teacher a question, Maya was aghast, "No! The camera would focus on me and EVERYONE would know that I didn't understand something!" She recalled how her friends would redirect her when she was not paying attention in the classroom. For example, one sitting near her would cue her, pick up her book, and read by pointing at hers. Maya said, "I just can't feel them that way on the screen."

DOI: 10.4324/9781003284741-2

Interest is a powerful motivator that can foster learning and enhance attention. Using a student's interests can guide an educational therapist's interventions so that greater focus, sustained attention, and reengagement are promoted. Content that features or builds on a student's interests can create greater engagement and motivation particularly for a student who is "unmotivated or reluctant" (Hidi, S. and Berndorff, D., 1998; Hidi, S. and Harackiewicz, J. M., 2000; Harackiewicz et al., 2016).

Research has shown that emotional engagement in learning is critical; when learning is connected to an area of interest, it becomes more meaningful and relevant (Immordino-Yang & Faeth, 2016). A student will read *more* when motivated by *interest* and choice of topic (Guthrie et al., 2000; Hirsch, E. D., Jr., 2003). By reading more, a student's background knowledge and vocabulary increase (Cullinan, 2000; Juel, 1990). Having adequate background knowledge influences how well a student comprehends the text. (Wexler, 2019; Kaefer et al., 2015; Recht & Leslie, 1988). Research has also shown that what appears to be a gap in comprehension may not be an issue with *skills* but may be gaps in *knowledge* (Wexler, 2019; Kaefer et al., 2015; Recht & Leslie, 1988). This research guided much of my thinking about how to engage Maya.

Student effort is a **matter of choice**. Effort is more readily available in areas of marked interest. Interest allows learning to be maintained, deepen, and segue into other content (Begin, 1999; Krapp, 1999; Dweck, 2002). Maya's difficulties with attention were well-documented in the neuropsychologist's report. Engaging her was key. This was my plan for Maya – to determine how long she could attend and to engage her deeply in order to foster new learning, aid in retention of new learning, and create motivation to write. It became essential to discover Maya's interests and leverage them to create personalized instructional content. (See Figure 2.2, at the end of the chapter, to view an example of a Four Square Graphic Organizer Using Engagement Concepts.)

## Maya's Interests

I had gleaned that Maya was fascinated with Disneyland, Disney movies, and the online suite of games, Minecraft. I used "Minecraft" as our Zoom passcode, although I had never played it. By using an area of keen interest, I signaled that I was interested in her world. I asked her to describe a few of her favorite games. She was cast in the role of "the expert" and I was the novice learner; she thoroughly enjoyed the role reversal. I asked her, if she was going to write about a Minecraft game, how would she begin?

"I don't know", she replied.

"Do you have a writing process?" I asked.

"No. Not really", she said.

Early sessions were oral or employed a whiteboard held by each of us up to the computer's camera, as I did not want any possibility of her feeling uneasy by committing her work to paper. Maya enjoyed the use of her whiteboard and seemed particularly pleased that she could choose from an array of colored markers her mother had provided at my request.

I had not seen much of her writing yet. "Can you write about Minecraft for 3 minutes?" I asked.

I hoped that the very brief time frame would not overwhelm her. She dutifully wrote on her whiteboard for several lines but with few capital letters and no ending punctuation.

"Do you write in paragraphs?" I asked.

"Not really. I *can* write in paragraphs, but I don't know where to end them. They just go on and on until I run out of things to say."

"I don't see many capitals or periods." I had noted Maya would liberally sprinkle commas in place of ending punctuation creating long run-on sentences. She laughed when I gently called her the "Comma Queen."

"Why don't you use periods?" I asked.

"I thought commas worked", she answered and then added softly, "I don't really know where a sentence ends."

I replied that we would work on that and that a sentence was a complete thought. Likely, she had recently been instructed in using commas to create compound or complex sentences and was attempting to use them. But one cannot construct more complex sentences until basic sentences are mastered. I suggested that, in the next session, she tell me about one of her favorite Minecraft games and I would take notes.

## Organizing Her Ideas in Writing – The Four Square Approach

I had thought about the many excellent methodologies for teaching writing and decided to try using the Four Square Graphic Organizer Method first (Gould, 1999). Maya needed to learn what was a sentence, a paragraph, and how to organize her writing. From the neuropsychologist's report, she did not need grammar support or assistance in creating ideas, which were the benefits of other writing programs and tools.

The Four Square approach is a method of teaching basic writing skills that is applicable across many grade levels and curriculum areas. It is more than a stand-alone graphic organizer. It can be applied for writing a narrative, a description, expository, and persuasive forms of writing. All types of graphic organizers help students conceptualize, understand, and structure a piece of writing. There are many excellent ones and are most effective when matched to the exact intent of writing. Maya needed to learn how to structure a piece of written discourse successfully. By using the Four Square method, it could "grow" as her writing skills developed.

As Maya described her current favorite game, a simulation of Disneyland, I took bulleted notes, which I placed in a box on my whiteboard. Introducing Maya to the method, I carefully used "purposeful language" by stating that each bullet would become a "complete thought" since she was not sure about what a sentence was. She clearly enjoyed the process and teaching me about the wonders of the game. In subsequent sessions, she completed the three other quadrants describing other Minecraft games, placing "bullets" on her whiteboard. I specified that at least four bullets were needed for each quadrant, so that each quadrant would contain enough material to become a four-sentence paragraph. My whiteboard mirrored hers exactly, by using her wording and keeping to her exact order. Notice that I was managing cognitive load for her, in that I was managing the writing process and she was working on a topic of deep knowledge and interest.

Soon I directed Maya to choose one quadrant to "build out" (into a paragraph). Maya learned that each "complete thought" began with a capital letter and required ending punctuation. It was laborious work but she used one quadrant to create a well-constructed paragraph. Her new learning was carefully managed and required only the most basic writing mechanics.

## Each New Session

Sessions had a rhythm and each began with a check-in. I began by asking, "How are you?"

She always answered, "Good."

"What's happening in Maya-land?"

My question was a play on her fascination with Disneyland. Since she often was unguarded in her responses, I heard about her friends and how they were trying to stay connected without physically visiting each other, about the movies she was watching, and about school.

I asked if she had another place in her room (other than her bed) that might be better for writing. She obediently moved to a nearby desk. I began dictating simple sentences for her to write down and punctuate. I always used her name and those of her friends. This always "sparked" her *interest* and she would giggle as she wrote out each sentence. Her friends were important to her, galvanized her attention, and motivated her to write. To date, she had not capitalized proper nouns, so this practice was helpful. Sometimes I dictated an incomplete sentence like "The dog." She began to embrace the idea that if it was not "a complete thought" it was not a sentence.

## Creating a Vocabulary Ladder

Maya's vocabulary seemed limited. I told her she would be constructing a "word ladder." I drew a simple ladder on my whiteboard with broad steps on which to write words. I was attempting to show her that words had nuanced meanings. I asked her to think of words that meant *fun*. This was not easy for her. I waited patiently, not giving up. Eventually, she said *surprising* which was not exactly a synonym but I accepted it. Then, she listed *exciting*, *thrilling*, and *exhilarating*. So, she did have more vocabulary than she wrote or spoke. Good! Since the words were coming more easily now, I extended the task and my ladder in the opposite direction. I asked her to list words that meant *not fun*. She responded with an interesting array: *exhausting*, *boring*, *hard*, and *challenging*. We would return to this activity in future sessions.

## Gold Stars

In addition to reviewing punctuation rules and having her organize her experiences into paragraphs, I thought I should determine her spelling skills. The neuropsychological report noted she could spell words in isolation and I thought I should determine her skill level. I began assessing using a published list ranking those most commonly used by student writers and listed by grade level. The first 25 words are used in 33% of student writing; the first 100 words appear in 50% of student and adult writing; and the first 1,000 words are used in 89% of everyday writing (Sitton, 2006). Maya could spell correctly, in writing, most of the first 100 words. If she erred, she spelled phonetically. After she read back and spelled aloud each word correctly, I would comment. "Good. Right. Yes. Nice. etc." I had session activities organized into 10–15 minute "chunks." She could pay attention for that time span. In nearly every session, she began asking, "Can we take a spelling break?", which I thought meant she had focused for long enough, her attention was waning, and/or I had signaled a switch to another task but she was not ready for a transition. Or, perhaps her request merely indicated that she wanted to do something within the context of writing where she had adequate skills.

## Using the Four Square Method

When writing from her bulleted quadrant, she could create individual sentences. After writing each sentence, she would look back and add in capital letters and ending punctuation. Writing a sentence was a series of discrete tasks. If she did not know something, she would ask for help in a little girl's voice signaling her distress, also noted in the neuropsychologist's report. Sometimes she would ask how to spell a word and I would ask how she had written it. She was usually correct. Rather than merely giving her the answer, I was encouraging her to become more self-reliant.

Maya painstakingly wrote in her writing journal what she understood as her new writing process:

Pick your topic
put an idea in every box

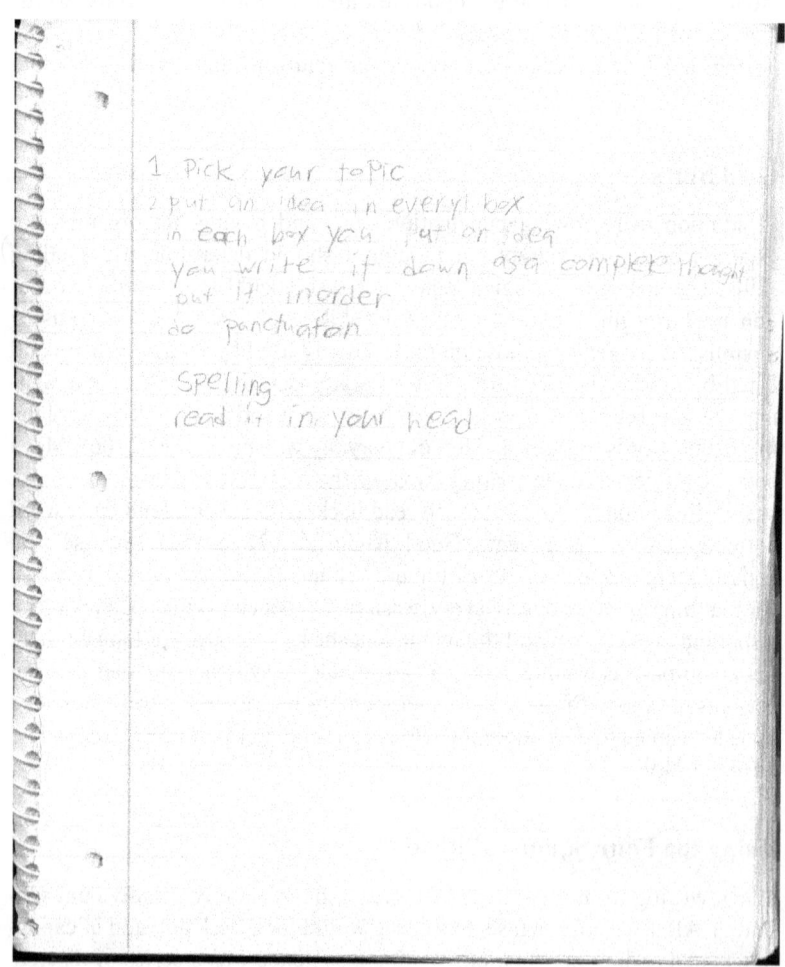

*Figure 2.1* Her Writing Process

in each box you put an idea
you write it down as a complete thought
put it in order
spelling
read it in your head

When she completed a second paragraph using her bullets describing the Minecraft game, Bed Wars, I said, "Gold Star, Maya!"

She beamed and held her hands high over her head, swaying as if dancing to music and chanting, "I earned a gold star! I earned a gold star!" Her exuberance was surprising. The reasons for needing praise became apparent in the upcoming IEP meeting.

## IEP Meeting for the IEE Process

After receiving the neuropsychologist's report, the parents sent the report to the school district and requested an IEP meeting. They asked that I attend the virtual meeting and present my analysis of her current level of functioning in writing. At this meeting, where the results of the IEE and my analysis were presented to school personnel, it became clear that my role would expand to include advocacy since I had first-hand knowledge of Maya's needs. I had successfully argued *why* the district's use of the Woodcock-Johnson-IV "Writing Samples" to "prove" that she could write at grade level, was misguided. I had pointed out that the "Writing Samples" requires only a single sentence response (not writing a multiple-paragraph essay, as her IEP goal indicated) and the scoring did not discount for any spelling, grammar, or punctuation errors. It was simply a wholly inappropriate measure.

The English teacher said she currently had an A- in that class. Knowing Maya's skills, that seemed impossible. I asked if her grade was awarded for the **content** of her writing assignments or for timely submissions. The teacher acknowledged that grades were awarded solely on whether work had been submitted. When the meeting was nearly over, the family asked for any evidence that Maya could independently write a multiple-paragraph essay, an IEP goal the district claimed she had met. The school could provide no evidence. The family's advocate asked that they agree to reinstate Maya's IEP. The district seemed intractable and stood by its decision to exit Maya from special education services. The advocate was obviously outraged and informed the district that the family had retained a special education lawyer and the family would "fight on." The family told me I was now in the dual role of advocate and ET.

Later, Maya told me she had never received **any** feedback for her work in English – just full credit for "turning everything in on time."

## Missing Fundamentals

It became increasingly clear that there were significant below-grade-level gaps in what Maya knew about the mechanics of writing. She did not begin a sentence with a capital letter, use ending punctuation, and confused plurals and possessives. Nor did she know where to place the apostrophe in a contraction. Maya did not know the difference between a noun, a verb, an adverb, or an adjective. Maya told me that her friends liked to play "mad libs" and thought her word choices were particularly hilarious.

It was interesting to this researcher to discover these gaps are skills taught and mastered in the 2nd–3rd grades. In the records review, it was revealed that Maya did not receive any special education services until the end of the 3rd grade. It appeared that these foundational skills never occurred or were confused.

Learning that is not well understood, or not clearly demarcated (delineated), can readily become confused or conflated. Those teaching early reading skills know that teaching the vowels sounds "short i" and "short e" can be easily confused, as they sound alike to many. So, teaching them is separated, creating demarcation. Maya confused plurals and possessives, likely because they had been taught too close together and before she understood the use of each. They were not demarcated in her learning. She did not know where to place an apostrophe in a contraction, nor what it stood for; "couldn't" was written as "could'nt." She did not have the concept that an apostrophe was placed where a letter or letters were purposefully left out. In not understanding the concept, she created her own meaning; an apostrophe was placed *between* the two words.

In each session, we followed a similar sequence of short tasks: 1) How are things in Maya-land? 2) A review of punctuation and capitalization rules retaught thus far. 3) Asking her to write a selection of the previous spelling words where each one was now written in a sentence. I noted whether she wrote in a complete sentence with a beginning capital letter and ending punctuation. 4) A specific writing task. 5) Asking her to edit what she had written as a separate process. 6) Having her read each sentence aloud and then reread the sentence stating the capitalization and ending punctuation. "In Capital D Disneyland you can go on rides period."

Originally, I asked her parents for an additional camera so that I could watch her write. When that was not forthcoming, because Maya objected that "it would be creepy", I looked for the small mirror attachment that would be placed on top of her computer screen so that I could view her writing as she worked (www.ipevo.com/products/mirror-cam). However, those devices were sold out and back-ordered for months. I had briefly considered having her use her cell phone camera as a document camera. (I had recently learned how to do this with my own phone.) However, this strategy was quickly discarded, given that Maya was reported to be highly distractable. I reasoned that having her read each sentence aloud voicing the capitalization and punctuation was good preparation for using voice-to-text software well. Maya was always cooperative.

However, as one session began, her mixed-type ADHD was clearly demonstrated for the first time. Maya was spinning around in her office chair. She spun faster and faster until I asked her to stop saying, "I'm going to be sick if you don't stop spinning." She complied but her hands were moving nonstop and she was humming her wordless songs aloud. Maya could not follow oral directions although she was gazing directly into the screen. Most alarmingly, she could not recall the comma rule about separating items in serial list with commas. She had appeared to have "mastered" this punctuation rule in the prior sessions. The session was simply a disaster. No new learning could occur since the recall of past sessions was unobtainable and her ability to focus was so limited. Very likely, this was the girl the neuropsychologist had met and described in her report. Later, I confirmed with her mother that Maya had been unmedicated when assessed and was

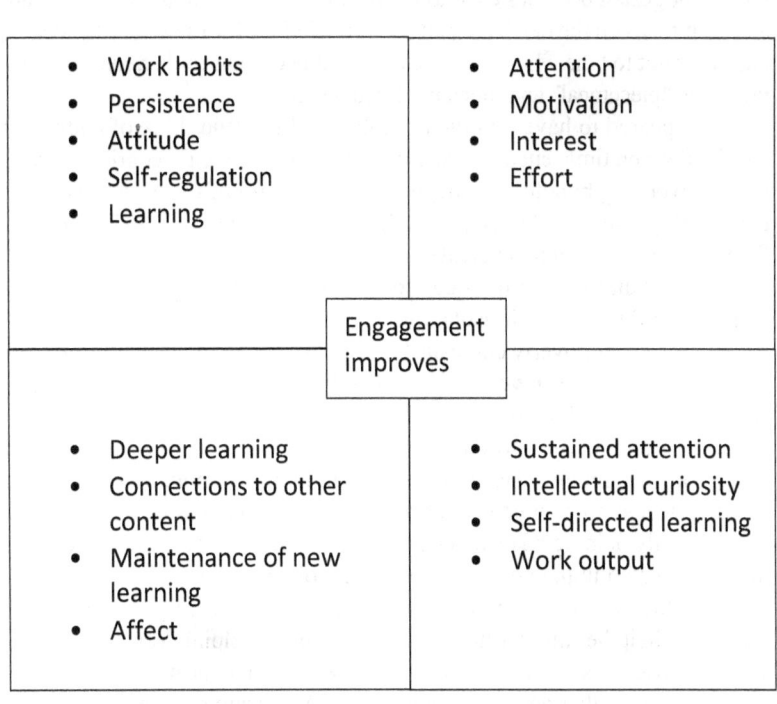

*Figure 2.2* Example of Four Square Graphic Organizer Using Engagement Concepts

unmedicated in this session. Previously, she had been medicated in all the prior sessions. Maya had decided that since virtual school "was a waste" she did not need to be medicated anymore.

## Summary

To date, I had learned that many of the fundamentals of written expression were missing or confused. Maya was responding well to the neuropsychological approaches that fostered interest, engagement, and sustained attention. A comfortable rhythm to each session had been established. "Chunking" the time we worked into smaller sections appeared to help counter her distractibility. She was responding well, too, to the use of the Four Square Graphic Organizer. It was assisting her in seeing how a sentence was constructed and how to link her sentences into a well-sequenced paragraph. Maya suggested a "spelling break" in every session and I wondered about the meaning of those requests. I was applying my process approach of observing and noting what was revealed with each new diagnostic task. I began to hypothesize that Maya's approach to learning was one of "parts to whole." Some learners focus on details until "the whole" or gestalt becomes clear to them. Others begin with the whole picture and then focus on the details or parts. I wondered if Maya saw only the details but never got to "the whole." If that was what occurring for her, new learning would be "piecemeal" and much harder to recall.

She appeared to have a limited vocabulary but could think of additional words, if given time, encouragement, and practice. I would continue to verify this working hypothesis. Maya reported her friends were accepting of her learning issues, endeavored to help her refocus in pre-COVID, (face-to-face) classes, and did not ridicule her.

I believed that Maya requested "spelling breaks" because it was a writing skill she could do well, in isolation, and she desired the simple reward of being praised. Her overly enthusiastic response to "earning a gold star" was startling. Likely, she craved validation and feedback for her efforts beyond acknowledgment of her on-time submissions.

As with the decision to hire me, Maya's opinions held a great deal of sway with her mother. Her mother was ambivalent about whether Maya actually needed to be medicated for ADHD and did not know if "the meds were actually helping." However, her mother told me that Maya had chosen to be medicated in the year prior when school was held in-person. I would hold firm that medication was essential, at least during her sessions with me. I hoped to help her mother understand its value in helping Maya learn. The school district was still intent on denying her special education services and I wondered how that decision would impact Maya and her family.

# References

Banna, J. et al. (2015). *Strategies to promote engaged learning in an online introductory nutrition course.* www.researchgate.net/publication/280532272_Interaction_matters_Strategies_to_promote_engaged_learning_in_an_online_introductory_nutrition_course/link/55c43db608aeca747d5fb61b/download

Begin, D. A. (1999). Influences on classroom interest. *Educational Psychologist, 34,* 87–98.

Cullinan, B. E. (2000). Independent reading and school achievement. *School Library Media Research, 3*(3), 1–24.

Dweck, C. (2002). The development of ability conceptions. In A. Wigfield & J. S. Eccles (Eds.), *Development of achievement motivation.* Academic Press.

Glossary of Educational Reform. (2016). *Definition of engagement.* Great Schools Partnership. www.edglossary.org/student-engagement/

Gould, J. S., & Gould, E. J. (1999). *Four square: Writing method for grades 7–9: A unique approach to teaching basic writing skills.* Teaching and Learning Company a Lorenz Company.

Guthrie, J. T., Wigfield, A., & VonSecker, C. (2000). Effects of integrated instruction on motivation and strategy use in reading. *Journal of Educational Psychology, 92*(2), 331–341.

Harakiewicz, J. et al. (2016). *Interest matters: The importance of promoting interest in education.* Interest Matters. www.ncbi.nlm.nih.gov/pmc/articles/PMC5839644/

Hidi, S., & Berndorff, D. (1998). Situational interest and learning. In L. Hoffmann, A. Krapp, K. A. Renninger, & J. Baumert (Eds.), *Interest and learning.* Institute for Science Education (IPN).

Hidi, S., & Harackiewicz, J. M. (2000). Motivating the academically unmotivated: A critical issue for the 21st century. *Review of Educational Research, 70,* 151–179.

Hirsch, E. D., Jr. (2003, Summer). Reading comprehension requires knowledge – of words and the world. *American Educator, 27*(1), 10–22, 28–29, 44.

Immordino-Yang, M. H., & Faeth, M. (2016). The role of emotion and skilled intuition in learning. In M. H. Immordino-Yang (Ed.), *Emotions, learning, and the brain* (pp. 93–105). W. W. Norton & Company.

*IPEVO Mirror-Cam.* www.ipevo.com/products/mirror-cam

Juel, C. (1990). Effects of reading group assignment on reading development in first and second grade. *Journal of Reading Behavior, 22*(3), 233–254.

Kaefer, T., Neuman, S. B., & Pinkham, A. M. (2015). Pre-existing background knowledge influences socioeconomic differences in preschoolers' word learning and comprehension. *Reading Psychology, 36*(3), 203–231.

Krapp, A. (1999). Interest, motivation, and learning: An educational-psychological perspective. *Learning and Information, 14*(1), 23–40.

Martin, F., & Bolliger, D. U. (2018). Engagement matters: Student perceptions on the importance of engagement strategies in the online learning environment. *Online Learning, 22*(1), 205–222. doi:10.24059/olj.v22i1.1092

Recht, D. R., & Leslie, L. (1988). Effect of prior knowledge on good and poor readers' memory of text. *Journal of Educational Psychology, 80*(1), 16–20.

Sitton, R. (2006). *List of 1200 high frequent spelling words.* https://az02204140.schoolwires.net/cms/lib/AZ02204140/Centricity/Domain/850/1200wordlist.pdf

Wexler, N. (2019). *The knowledge gap: The hidden cause of America's broken education system – and how to fix it.* Avery.

# 3 Writing Beyond Her Direct Experience

## October

Young writers write from their own experiential base – "about my dog, Teddy", "why I like playing soccer", and "what I did over the weekend." The teacher gives instruction in describing something well or in creating a clear beginning and end in one's writing. Students are not yet combining reading and writing. I wanted to begin extending Maya's writing beyond her own experiences, as the "next step" in her development. However, I wanted to use an area of *keen interest* to *motivate* her to read and write. She needed to move past the earlier stages of writing by combining reading with writing.

## Disneyland Is Closed Due to COVID-19

Because Maya was enamored of Disneyland, I emailed her mother a PDF of a recent article from the newspaper. It was a colorful drawing of Disneyland and detailed the kinds of changes the park might undertake to ensure public safety while reopening during the COVID-19 pandemic. I felt Maya could read it since most newspaper writers are careful to write at a 6th-grade readability or lower. I hoped Maya would be intrigued to learn what changes Disneyland, her "favorite place on the planet", was considering. She appeared to recoil at the length of the article (three pages with one being a colored map of the park).

She asked, "Do I have to read all of that? Could we take turns reading?"

This is one of the moments where a professional makes an immediate decision. I wanted her to read, take notes, and write. She would be accomplishing that if we alternated as readers.

"Yes. Fine", I answered.

She was able to readily restate the key points of the article. I asked her to set up the four boxes.

DOI: 10.4324/9781003284741-3

"What do I put in each one?" Maya asked.

"The first box can be why you like going to Disneyland. The second can be the reasons the park is closed."

"To keep people safe." She began writing bullets for those.

"The third can be the information in the article you just read."

"The changes?"

"Does that seem to go next?" Maya nodded. Later, she converted her "bullets" from each box into sentences. Sentences began with a capital letter. Good.

"Does Disneyland need a capital?" asked Maya.

Capitalizing proper nouns was reviewed. Few sentences had ending punctuation even after my request to edit her work.

"I see that sentences begin with a capital letter. Good. You have turned all of your bullets into complete thoughts. Very good. But most of the sentences do not end with a period."

Maya shrugged.

"Is it because it is too hard to think about all of those things at once?" another shrug was her response. So, I changed tactics.

Maya had shoulder-length dark brown hair. It was always neatly styled. I asked Maya if anyone had to remind her to comb her hair in the morning.

"No! Of course not!"

"Why not?" I asked.

"That's just silly", she answered. "I just do it!"

"What is the difference between a habit and something new that you are just learning?"

She pondered this and replied, "A habit is something you don't have to think about. You just do it."

"Ah . . . you are going to have to practice enough that capitals and periods become a habit. Okay?" I asked gently.

"Okay", she whispered back.

## Reading From Winnie the Pooh and Visualization

Maya said she enjoyed the *Winnie the Pooh* movie and it seemed she had memorized much of the dialogue by frequent viewings. I asked if she had ever read the stories and held up my hardbound copy.

She exclaimed, "Oh! It's a book?"

"Have you ever seen this book before?"

"No. Well, maybe. I think I saw a group of them in a bookstore window once."

"Do you remember being read other books?"

"No", answered Maya nonchalantly.

I read aloud a selection from the book, holding up the pictures to the camera. She pronounced it quite different from the movie. Thinking I could improve her reading comprehension by strengthening her visualization skills, I took her through a series of visualization exercises loosely based on Nanci Bell's Visualizing and Verbalizing® Language program. Much to my surprise, Maya could create images easily and could visualize a topic sentence. She patiently did each exercise. When I praised her, I told her that she would be working toward "making movies" when she read.

Maya calmly announced, "I can already do that."

I asked her to visualize a passage, as I read it, and then describe her visualizations to me. Maya responded in great detail. This was a skill she did not need to be *taught*. It was an important skill she needed to learn to *use*.

## Establishing the Learning Purpose

Sessions had a familiar cadence. After the "What's happening in Maya-land question", I would lay out the session's agenda and I usually planned for each task to last 10–15 minutes after the check-in. I remembered an important neuropsychological principle in learning – that learning is accomplished more readily if the learning purpose is clearly stated and understood by the student. This helps to *focus* and orient the learner. It also *cues recall* for what is already known about a subject or topic and elicits past learning. A clear learning purpose (or goal) signals not only the topics or tasks to be covered but it clarifies what will be the same and what will be new learning (creating better demarcation). Or, what is mostly the same and will be expanded upon. Since Zoom features a visual format, a shift between tasks and topics may not be as readily apparent as when I reached across the table to get a book or pulled out a piece of prior writing from a student's notebook. For a student with ADHD, being clear about the session's learning purposes and goals, at the outset, is important. In Maya's case, it was essential; it assisted in reminding her about her recent work on writing mechanics. I had been stating the session's agenda orally.

In face-to-face educational therapy, it was always written on a whiteboard in my office for each student. I realized that I had missed this step with Maya. Since discovering she approached learning in a visual mode, my verbal agenda was not adequate. I began writing the agenda, in advance, on Zoom's whiteboard and used a different color for each item. Although not a robust tool, it was adequate for this simple task. If she appeared tired (as she often played video games until 2 am), I crossed out the items as she completed them, to give her a sense of accomplishment. If Maya appeared anxious or distracted at the outset, I allowed her to choose the order of the work. This simple gesture of appearing to cede power usually propelled her into the learning mode. I realized I needed to replicate *all* of the things I had done in face-to-face educational therapy to be effective. Over time, I dictated the agenda to her and she wrote it down. She took genuine pleasure in crossing out items as she completed them or in choosing the order of the session's activities.

## Reading and Writing from ReadWorks Articles

Maya liked animals. She often appeared on screen holding a stuffed animal that she would introduce to me. "This is Chirp," she said, holding up a penguin.

I began having her read short articles that I had reviewed and selected from ReadWorks (readworks.org). Articles can be searched by topic, grade, or Lexile level. Currently, there are 4,560 kindergarten–12th-grade texts which have vocabulary, multiple-choice, or open-ended questions and many have audible versions. Fortunately, Maya clearly stated that she "hated" listening to recorded "robot voices" and would read aloud. Each article was chosen because it linked to one of her interests. Maya approached each article willingly and read about sharks, sea otters, puffins, and penguins (a nod to Chirp).

Now, Maya was reading with the express purpose of reading for meaning, understanding what she read, and not just to sound fluent. It became immediately clear that she could answer all the multiple-choice questions correctly by eliminating obviously incorrect answers. So, I began creating open-ended questions that required inferential thinking or the use of a new vocabulary word instead. I required that she write her responses to each question. The tasks alternated between answering the prepared questions or taking bulleted notes and writing a summary. She could recall all of the relevant facts but struggled to create a summary – even orally. The main idea was never clear to her; this replicated the neuropsychologist's comments about Maya's reading skills and my previous observations. Finally, with repeated guided practice visualizing key terms in her notes and repeatedly asking her what they have in common, she could create a verbal summary and, later, a written one. In her written summary about the endangered status of the Black-Footed Penguins, she wrote five simple sentences but each was a "complete thought." All words were spelled correctly and her sentences began with a capital letter in four out of five of the sentences.

However, when I added a new dimension, creating a concluding sentence, the final period was missing and Maya grumbled, "Why do I have to write it again? I already said it!"

I had pushed a little too quickly by adding in a new writing component since she had seemed to be doing so well. In our eagerness to have students succeed, Educational Therapists can misjudge the pace and demand of new learning when successful practice would have been more beneficial.

## When Not Medicated

The sessions where Maya was unmedicated were limited in how much new learning could be accomplished. While she was not always physically active, she had great difficulty in recalling recently accomplished work where she had appeared to have "mastered" something in her writing skills. Less-observable internal distractions must have been occurring, as she always missed transitions between activities, even while staring at the screen. I recalled that the neuropsychologist had made specific mention that Maya could be staring directly at the screen but was not focusing her attention on it. This was occurring.

"Wait. Wait! What? I'm supposed to get my notebook?"

When I alerted her mother and strongly recommended that Maya be medicated for our sessions, she agreed to discuss it with the doctor. They decided that Maya would take a short acting stimulant (Ritalin) at noon on the days we worked together. Goodness knows what Maya got out of her virtual day at school, but I was willing to accept this compromise.

## Science Research Paper

Maya rarely shared anything about school. I came to understand that she compartmentalized aspects of her life and our work was in a discrete space separate from school. So, I was quite surprised when she exclaimed in a panicky voice, "I need your help! I have to write a 3 to 5 page research paper about viruses and I have never ever written anything longer than 2 pages. AND it was only 2 pages because I used a huge font!" Maya's panic was evident and brought into question the district's assertion that she had met all of her IEP goals, including the ability to independently plan and write a multiple-paragraph essay. The research paper was due in a few days.

"How much research have you done?"

"None", was her frank admission.

"Then we'd better get started."

She had an online science text she was to use. I asked her to screenshare it with me and she began reading the text. I noticed it was clearly organized into topics with each section demarcated by bold headings but she was skipping over each heading.

I asked, "Why aren't you reading the bold headings?"

She answered that they were "in the way."

"Hmm. I think they are important. It costs more to make a text with illustrations and bold print. They are there to guide the reader, to let you know what is going to be presented in that section."

"Oh", she replied, and started again, this time reading the headings aloud.

"How are you going to organize the information?"
"I don't know", she replied plaintively.
"You can set up boxes for each topic."
"What do I put in each box?"
"Look back at the headings."
"Oh! I see. What is a virus? How do they replicate? What are some of the viruses that make people sick? About COVID. That part is not in the book but I can find it from a government source; you have to refer to a government source for good information."

She titled her four squares and painstakingly searched for information to create bullets in each section.

In the next session, she had made good progress researching and filling in bullets for each square. She had just located an "approved" CDC.gov site about COVID-19. As she read aloud, she included reading each bold heading.

I was feeling confident that she now understood the importance of the headings so I asked, "Maya, why should you read the headings?"

"To guide the reader", she answered promptly. I felt pleased; then I thought it sounded a little bit too much like what I had told her so I asked, "Maya, who is the reader?"

"I have no idea."

So much for a lesson learned. Being an educational therapist is very, very humbling, at times.

## IEP Meeting Attended by Maya's Family's Lawyer

Maya's family removed the advocate and hired a lawyer skilled in special education disagreements and she would attend all future IEP meetings. Since a "stay put" order was in effect, their lawyer asked the district to reinstate the legal requirements of new annual goals. The district restated that Maya had met all of her goals. That prompted the family's lawyer to request that I write "realistic goals" which would be presented to the school district team at the next IEP meeting. I reviewed the Common Core Standards for English Language Arts (www.corestandards.org/ELA-Literacy/RL/4/ grades 2–4, wrote a brief overview of her current writing status based on our work and wrote Maya-specific goals). The goals addressed these standards:

CCSS.ELA-LITERACY.W.3.1.C
Use linking words and phrases (e.g., *because, therefore, since, for example*) to connect opinions and reasons.
CCSS.ELA-LITERACY.W.3.1.D
Provide a concluding statement or section.

CCSS.ELA-LITERACY.L.4.1
Demonstrate command of the conventions of standard English capitalization, punctuation, and spelling when writing.
CCSS.ELA-LITERACY.L.4.2.A
Use correct capitalization.
CCSS.ELA-LITERACY.L.4.2.B
Use commas and quotation marks to mark direct speech and quotations from a text.
CCSS.ELA-LITERACY.L.4.2.C
Use a comma before a coordinating conjunction in a compound sentence.
CCSS.ELA-LITERACY.L.4.1.F
Produce complete sentences, recognizing and correcting inappropriate fragments and run-ons.

They were submitted in advance of the meeting. At the meeting, the school team listened politely but immediately dismissed them. The most telling comment was made by the resource specialist who said, "But these are below grade level."

I said I realized that but they reflected where Maya was currently functioning.

The resource specialist replied, "But who is going to teach her these skills?"

"I thought you might", was my response.

"Oh no! That is not my job."

I asked respectfully, "Then, what is your job? When I was a resource specialist, I believed that *was* my job."

"Oh no", she responded as if I was out of touch with schools and special education law, in particular. "My job is to ensure a student has access to the general curriculum."

I replied, "Using software such as Grammarly (www.grammarly.com/) while you *instruct* Maya to develop her writing skills may be a useful accommodation. Giving a student an audiobook so that she may listen to the textbook is a useful accommodation while you are *teaching* that student to read. Instruction and teaching would be my goals as a resource specialist."

The meeting had been recorded by both sides. It was over. The family's lawyer stated, for the record, that the family had attempted voluntary mediation, was willing to keep meeting if the district had anything new to offer, and would pursue arbitration, if necessary. (www.cde.ca.gov/sp/se/qa/hearmedac cgdlns.asp). After the meeting, the family, the lawyer, and I held a "debriefing" via Zoom. I asked about the claim that a resource specialist was only responsible for giving students "access to the curriculum" but not direct instruction or remediation. She answered that this was not correct and the district was "failing Maya" and as a result the family should seek reimbursement for all of my sessions if they proceeded to arbitration. She sent a link to understand this point of law (https://sites.ed.gov/idea/files/policy_speced_guid_idea_memosdcltrs_guidance-on-fape-11-17-2015.pdf). On it was a very clear example that "specialized instruction" was required to improve specific "deficit areas" while accommodations were also supplied to access the general education curriculum.

## Summary

To date, I had learned many essential things. Maya could not recall being read to as a child. Maya's difficulties in stating the "main idea" or in creating a topic sentence were related. She had been reading "to sound fluent" but comprehending only at a surface level. She could recall some information but could not determine the main idea and confused supporting details with the main idea. Maya could glean the details, "the parts", but struggled with understanding "the whole." Summarization is nearly impossible without comprehending the main idea.

Learning to summarize is a 4th-grade skill and likely related to her ignoring the bold headings and difficulties with "parts to whole." I surmised that she had missed instruction on summarization or had not understood the intent of that practice in the 3rd and 4th grades. Reading and writing are related skills and there was much work to be done with Maya. She could visualize exceptionally well but did not understand how that skill could be applied to her reading. I would request that she "visualize" headings and topic sentences in the text as a strategy to aid her understanding of the main idea. I realized that using a visual mode to provide a clear agenda for each session's work and to clarify new learning goals was essential. Importantly, I discovered that a "medicated Maya" was a vastly different learner than the unmedicated one.

Additionally, I was informed that her family had hired a well-regarded "special education" lawyer. They had requested a hearing with the California Office of Administrative Hearings. That department assigns a mediator to help the parties resolve the matter and, if that fails, an administrative law judge hears the case (https://edsource.org/2021/how-california-plans-to-deter-costly-special-education-disputes/658226). Maya's family had determined they would "fight on." Although I was not privy to all of the strategy meetings with the lawyer, I was now a part of the legal challenge – with all IEP meetings being recorded and conducted virtually!

# References

Bell, N. (2008). *Visualizing and verbalizing* (2nd ed.). Gander Publishing Co.
Common Core Standards for English Language Arts. www.corestandards.org/ELA-Literacy grades 2–4
EdSource. (2021). *How California plans to deter costly special education disputes.* https://edsource.org/2021/how-california-plans-to-deter-costly-special-education-disputes/658226
Grammarly. (2022). *Grammarly.* www.grammarly.com/
ReadWorks. (2022). www.readworks.org/
US Department of Education OSERS Policy Guidance on Free Appropriate Education. https://sites.ed.gov/idea/files/policy_speced_guid_idea_memosdcltrs_guidance-on-fape-11-17-2015.pdf

# 4 More Sustained Reading and Writing

### November–December

**Establishing New IEP Goals**

In response to our last meeting, the district had hired a lawyer specializing in special education disputes and I was directed by her to create new goals and benchmarks since Maya's IEP was out-of-date but was still required during the "stay put" period had been invoked. I had been forewarned by the family's lawyer to be prepared to suggest an assessment instrument other than the Woodcock-Johnson IV Tests of Achievement (WJ IV ACH). At that meeting, I recommended using the Wechsler Individual Achievement Test® Fourth Edition (WIAT-4) since the WJ IV ACH had been used previously and the neuropsychologist had just given the TOWL- 4. However, the district had not purchased the WIAT 4 yet and argued that they would buy it "within the year allowed" but that would be too late for establishing a current benchmark. So, we all agreed to their administering the Wechsler Individual Achievement Test® Third Edition (WIAT®-III) and the district agreed to share a copy of the protocol. (I had requested the WIAT 4 because the essay could be scored by a computer and the scoring would be objective rather than subjective, as can occur when scoring the WIAT®-III). When the family had a copy of her written essay, I would rescore it using the WIAT 4 software, since the writing prompt was exactly the same.

The district's proposed goals were generally along the lines of those I had presented and stated markers for evaluating writing in complete sentences and using proper mechanics including spelling and punctuation. It was stated that Maya would be able to organize and write a multiple-paragraph essay. It was unclear to me if the district was just "going through the motions" or if the mediation process was actually working.

## Sustained Reading and Writing

Maya used commas frequently and in places of ending punctuation. I had been gradually instructing her in their correct usage. To date, she had practiced with placing them in: three things in a series; an introductory phrase; appositives; an introductory word; direct names; and after an adverb clause that introduces a sentence. She had gained skills by creating her own sentences using her friends, as I had done earlier. Now, I wanted to move Maya beyond reading and answering questions based on the ReadWorks passages to a more sustained topic. Students in the middle school read longer texts and novels. To date, she had been reading relatively short passages with me. I thought of her interest in Disney characters and knew that there were hundreds of versions of the Cinderella story, the oldest being the Chinese ninth-century tale, Yen-Shen. Nearly every culture has a Cinderella-like story. The French story by Charles Perrault is over 300 years old and is the one closest to the Disney movie (www.ala.org/aboutala/offices/resources/multicultural). I hoped that, if Maya was intrigued by this, she could read a variety of the tales, take notes, and ultimately write an essay comparing two of her favorites. I was anticipating expanding her worldview beyond Disney and have her read in a genre, fairytales.

Fortunately, I had been preparing materials for this work because Maya came to the session in a very grumpy mood, although she had said that things were "good" (as always) in Maya-land. So, I said, "Let's change things up today. Let's begin with spelling." She nodded. I began reciting, "Spell the contraction for *do not*; spell the contraction for *is not;* spell the contraction for *where is;* spell the contraction for *it will;* spell *prince*."

"What?"

"Spell prince."

"Okay."

"Spell contraction for *she is*. Spell *carriage*."

"What? What's going on?" she asked.

"You'll see. Spell the contraction for *I am*. Spell *slipper*."

"What? What's going on?" demanded Maya.

"Spell *pumpkin*."

"This is all about Cinderella! What is going on?"

## Cinderella to Yeh-Shen

Now, clearly intrigued and with rapt attention, Maya listened as I described the project (the learning purpose) and asked her to tell me all she knew about Cinderella. She recalled that Cinderella was a poor girl, had a cruel stepmother, mean stepsisters, had to work hard, had a fairy godmother, went to the ball, met the prince, lost her slipper, had tiny feet, and married the prince. I had Maya write those items down creating a column for country of origin, characters, magic agent, plot, etc. to prepare for comparing each story.

Realizing that Maya had a keen interest in visual images, I found an illustrated video reading of Yeh-Shen to introduce the stories she would compare. I asked her to listen with good recall of the characters and events to place on her chart. Yeh-Shen is nearly starving but still shares her daily handful of rice with a magical carp in a nearby pond. It is her only friend. When her evil stepmother kills and eats the carp to punish Yeh-Shen, the bones of the magical carp help her prepare for a festival where she meets a handsome rich suitor. "The carp is the fairy godmother!" Maya exclaimed as she added that detail to her chart. I asked her to use her chart to write a summary of the story and challenged her "to develop *the habit* of writing sentences with capitals and ending punctuation." I reviewed using quotation marks for direct speech in dialogue and about starting a new line when a different character was speaking.

Maya wrote for 12 minutes; the longest time span to date. "Want to hear what I said so far?"

She read it out to me.

"Perfect!" was my response.

"Should I keep going?"

"Do you need a spelling break?" I asked.

"No! I'm writing!"

"Are you using your notes or just remembering?"

"Some of each", she responded. "Don't lose your glass slippers", the fish told her. "That's my favorite part!" she giggled.

She was still absorbed in writing. I noted good concentration. I asked if she wanted to edit it before sending a screenshot to me. "No, I remembered the challenge. Should I send it all to you?" (Maya would send me her work for review by taking a screenshot and emailing it to me.)

Next, she read the most familiar French version (Disney-esque) which delighted her. I noted she did not ask me to "partner read" with her for the first time. As she read aloud, she eagerly remarked upon the similarities and differences between this tale and the Disney movie. She filled in her comparison chart.

"Could you write comparing the Yeh-Shen and the French Cinderella versions of Cinderella?" She nodded emphatically.

"Don't try to sneak in the Disney one!" I gently teased her.

Maya wrote steadily for more than 23 minutes. I rarely interrupted her since she seemed so intent on the task. Instead, I logged in the minutes clicking by and thinking, "I am being paid to sit here!" She read me sections of what she had written at various intervals. She began with a topic sentence stating that the French Cinderella and the Chinese Cinderella were "very similar" but also "very different." Maya listed the similarities as the evil stepmom, losing the slippers, both of the fathers died, both had "animal sidekicks", both are pretty, and both of the stories had magic.

Occasionally, she asked a question.

"Is 'soon' one of those *time words?*"

"Is it?" I asked rather than just telling her.

"Yes, so it needs a comma" was her answer. (She had previously noted that many beginning prepositional phrases indicated a time – soon, after dinner, during the night, etc.) Ultimately the sentence Maya created was "Soon, Yeh Shen was ready to go to the festival wearing this beautiful [*sic*] blue dress and stunning gold slippers."

Nearing the end of the session, she said triumphantly, "I'm done! It's a page long!"

Upon review, Maya **had** written a full page with only one run-on sentence and included the required capital letters. Her use of quotation marks, commas, and contractions were all correct. Some words were misspelled (exacte/exact; befor/before; beutiful/beautiful; and sometimes Yeh-Shen was spelled Yeih Shen and not hyphenated) but many words were correct (devastated, festival, stunning, civilian, merchant, thought). Maya had captured all the essential details and summarized the Yeh-Shen story well. I thought, she is writing! And, if this continued through the subsequent Cinderella stories, Maya may have turned a corner in developing her writing skills.

## Chinye and Aschenputtel

Next, she read the African tale, Chinye, but dismissed it in her summary thusly, "I do not consider this a Cinderella story because it doesn't have the key points of Cinderella." This was a "rags to riches" story. She reluctantly agreed it might be considered a folk tale but certainly **not** a Cinderella story because "It didn't have a prince!" I believed we had concluded comparing stories but Maya asked, "What about the Grimm one? Could we read that?"

"Have you ever read it before?"

"No."

"Why do you want to add that in?"

"Because it's really bloody!"

Interestingly, this was the first time Maya had initiated something she wanted to explore, so, of course, we would read Grimm's story of Aschenputtel.

## Writing Using Transition Words

Maya no longer asked me to partner read with her. She was delighted by what she termed "the most disturbing Cinderella story." I told her she could take notes in the Four Square boxes or "storyboard" them, laying out the sequence of events in boxes horizontally. She chose the latter, which allowed me to introduce the notion of adding time-signal words to her writing – first, next, then, later, and finally. As she read aloud, I realized that she often asked insightful and analytical questions. To some, they may have seemed "random" or tangential, but I began to praise her for them because she was "reading for meaning" and applying logical reasoning. For example, in the Grimm version, the stepsisters wanted to fit into the tiny shoes to claim the prince's affection. The first stepsister cut off her toes to fit into the shoes; the second, her heel. As the prince mounted his horse with each of the stepsisters, in turn, the prince was alerted to the bleeding by the cries of a dove.

Maya exclaimed, "Couldn't he see her foot was bleeding?" And then, "Not again! That shoe must be really bloody by now!"

Her 2 ½ pages summarized the story well and utilized the words "next" and "finally." Maya wrote in complete sentences and punctuated all the sentences correctly, including contractions. Most words were spelled correctly; however, she confused plurals with possessives.

Despite my initial attempt at untangling these concepts, she remained confused. In our practice with plurals and possessives, she asked, "Where does the apostrophe go in the sentence The girls purse is blue? We know it's hers! and Jake has two dogs. They are *his* dogs right? So, dogs needs an apostrophe."

She was willing to attempt writing a concluding paragraph stating that the stories were "very different", as some were "more creative" than the others, and that the German version was her favorite as it was "the most disturbing and interesting one."

All combined, her Cinderella summaries and comparisons totaled 5 ½ pages of writing. As she looked at her writing notebook, she said in an awed tone, "This is the most I have ever written."

I responded with, "How does that feel Maya?"

She fisted her hands over her head and pumped them in the air.

I said, "I am proud of you. And, I want you to be proud of yourself." She nodded. I said, "It is raining gold stars." Her hands unclenched and she stood up grabbing the gold stars as if they were raining down on her.

## Summary

To date, I had learned that Maya could become engaged in reading within the fairy tale genre. Verification of this engagement was demonstrated by her no longer asking me to "partner read" with her. I surmised that moving from an area of interest and her background knowledge allowed her to write more than ever before while demonstrating much-improved use of writing mechanics. Her dysgraphia was obvious in her letter formation but did not hamper the amount she could write at any one session. When deeply engaged, she did not need "spelling breaks" and, for the first time, seemed delighted in her own writing. Evidence of her unique analytical thinking emerged. I did not view her questions as "random" but as verification that she was deeply engaged in the text.

Writing a summary is a skill introduced in the 4th grade (Common Core Standards English Language Arts Standards-Reading: Literature-Grade 4) so I was attempting to advance her writing closer to grade-level expectations. Summarizing is not merely a "retelling" of a story, but, instead, involves the ability to select main ideas and focus on key components, an area of difficulty for Maya. Again, Maya noted details which did not necessarily aggregate into a gestalt for her. Creating a comparison chart allowed Maya to write a summary while noting crucial features across multiple texts. Even though she dismissed the African tale as not being a "true Cinderella story", she was able to explain her reasoning in writing, another 4th-grade standard. Finally, Maya made the request to read the Grimm's tale. I hoped this signaled that Maya was becoming invested in her own learning and moving beyond merely being cooperative. I wondered if this initiative would persist.

I learned the district and family's lawyers had been negotiating. Although the district agreed to the WIAT III assessment, they informed the family they would not be assessing her "until the end of the summer" with no rationale for the delay provided. This appeared disingenuous to Maya's family and I was informed that they were planning to proceed with mediation and then onto arbitration, which is a trial, if necessary.

## References

Common Core Standards English Language Arts Standards-Reading: Literature-Grade 4 retrieved from www.corestandards.org/ELA-Literacy/RL/4/

Multi-national Cinderella stories www.ala.org/aboutala/offices/resources/multicultural

# 5 Applying Other Strategies

## Mid-December–January

### Notetaking to Improve Writing

Having piqued Maya's interest with the multinational Cinderella stories, I sought something that would sustain her interest in and past the winter holidays. Next, she should practice notetaking from a variety of sources. I chose another folklore area, Scandinavian gnomes called Tomtar (plural of Tomte). They seemed appropriately seasonal, are guardians of the rural farms, children, and animals, are mischievous, can be a bit naughty, and are always secretive. I thought that might appeal to Maya's interest in what she termed "twisted stories." For example, she was thrilled with the Grimm's detail that the dove "pecked out the step-sister's eyes" as punishment. After some research, I found many good resources about Tomtar and began the new unit with a "dark video", which had eerie music, no words but many evocative pictures of Tomtar skulking around in the stark rural landscape. I told Maya she was starting a new project.

"Why am I watching *this*? What are these things? Elves? Elf-gnomes? They are kinda creepy", she whispered in a delighted voice, as she watched.

I asked her to write a list of words that described the scenes, correcting her spelling when needed. Then, I asked Maya to watch the video again, specifically noting where the Tomtar lived, what work they seemed to do, how they looked, and how they seemed to act. I instructed her to create those headings in a notetaking format. She watched again, eagerly leaning forward and taking notes. "Do you need to watch it again?"

"No, I'm good", was her confident answer and she was right; she had captured the setting and the essential details.

DOI: 10.4324/9781003284741-5

## School Required Reading

However, things were not going as well in "Maya-land." She missed her friends terribly; her English class was required to read *Walk Two Moons*. She was clearly disinterested in that book. "It's SOOO boring, so I don't remember much", was her frank appraisal. I asked how many chapters they were required to read each week.

"Oh, I'm not reading it", she explained. "I am listening to it. I have an audiobook."

I was a bit surprised since she could read fluently (if not always with good comprehension) but tried not to let my face or voice reflect that.

"Why do you have an audiobook, Maya? Does everyone?" I thought it might be a response to handling course materials during COVID-19.

"No, just me. I always have audiobooks. I haven't had a book since the end of 3rd grade", she stated matter-of-factly.

I was shocked but strove to hide that. "Do you have any books at home that you read on your own?"

"No."

"Okay. Just listening to an audiobook can be hard. It can be hard to concentrate and remember. Do you visualize when you listen?"

"No", was Maya's honest response.

"Can you try that with the next chapter? You can visualize really well. It might help you understand and remember more about the book."

"I guess."

"Please try and let me know how it goes."

At the outset of beginning my work with Maya, I had set aside 15 minutes a week to check-in by phone with Maya's mother, at an agreed-upon day and time. This was something I had never done before, but she had seemed so anxious about the findings of the neuropsychological report and the legal challenge that I reasoned that having regular updates might be very helpful for her parent(s). That week, I asked her mother if she knew that Maya was not actually reading any books and had not read any since the end of the 3rd grade. Her mother was unaware and frankly surprised. I said that Maya and I would work on that in the future.

At the next session, I asked Maya if she had tried visualizing while she listened to the recording of *Walk Two Moons*. She said she had tried and "it helped a little bit" but "Sal (the main character) is lame. I know she misses her mother but the story goes on and on without any action. It's boring", was her verdict.

"How does your teacher check to see if you are understanding the story?"

"We have to answer really simple questions", Maya replied derisively.

"Can you show me?"

"Sure", said Maya, getting into her school portal, as I made her co-host so she could screenshare with me. "See. Short answers and fill in the blanks. Not really *writing*", she judged. A surprising comment comes from the student who now thinks that filling in the blanks is **not** writing.

## They Don't Care

She was correct in describing that lengthy writing was not required. However, I was shocked by the quality of her work but tried not to display that. Her answers had no capital letters – not to begin a sentence and not for the characters' names. Common words were misspelled, words I knew she *could* spell. And, there was no ending punctuation for many of her sentences.

I gently asked her why those things were missing since I knew she could include them in her writing now.

She shrugged and answered candidly, "Because they don't care."

I felt so sad for so many reasons. Her teachers seemed to still be grading only on timely submissions. How awful to feel that the quality of your responses and the thoughtfulness of your answers did not matter. And, how could I get Maya to generalize her developing writing skills into her school work and develop a *habit* if it did not seem to matter to anyone but me?

At the next check-in with her mother, I described what I had seen and what Maya had told me.

Since Maya was very engaged in writing with me, I asked for permission to check in with her resource specialist. I emailed a copy of the Release of Information to the school and arranged a time to speak to the resource specialist. She stated that Maya was "writing well" in class. So, I asked her to elaborate on that statement. She said that Maya had just written "an entire paragraph, with capitals and periods." However, Maya "had not capitalized names or proper nouns and she was not writing in advanced sentence structures, as was the expectation for the class." I asked her to describe Maya's writing. She responded that Maya was writing in simple sentences with run-ons. I asked what was Maya's attitude about writing? The resource specialist indicated she had checked with the English teacher who couldn't really "read" Maya since she was using an avatar, along with two-thirds of the class.

I asked, "What about Maya's attitude in the Resource class period? What had the resource specialist observed in Maya's work?" She responded that it was hard to gauge Maya's daily work since she was primarily assisting with homework completion and Maya turned her work in on time.

Then she shared, "The kids don't turn on their camera during Resource, so I can't really know how they are doing." More shocking news. Good teaching is always a recursive act. Plan. Teach. Observe. Question. Respond. Redirect or reteach, as necessary. Personally, I simply could not imagine any "teaching" that did not involve careful observation and evaluation of whether the instruction was being effective. I was sorely disheartened.

## Tomtar

In our sessions, Maya eagerly read the articles I supplied on Tomtar. She carefully added to her notes, made observations, and asked interesting questions.

> So, they are mischievous? They turned the milk sour? They sit on someone's head and give them a headache if the farmer and wife are not kind to the children or farm animals? That's good because they live way out in the country and no one would ever know. Does a Tomte ever get lonely? Why doesn't he let the farmer see him? Why are there never any woman Tomtar? How long do they live? Ohhhh this article says they may bite if they get REALLY mad! Is the bite poisonous? Could someone die from being bitten?

In another article, she learned that, when Christianity came to Scandinavia, the rural farm's protective Tomte merged with Father Christmas and brought a gift to each child. "Do Tomtar have a tiny sleigh and tiny reindeer?" About this time, her mother began decorating their home for Christmas. Maya wandered into the guest bedroom and gasped, "We have a Tomte in our house!" I had not anticipated that the Tomte would become a decorating fad that season; they appeared everywhere and that only added to Maya's excitement. But suddenly, she told me she was worried because her grandmother was going to stay in the room with the Tomte. Would it sit on her grandmother's head? Would it pull her hair in the night? Maya vowed to do **everything** to please the house Tomte; she added porridge to her mother's weekly shopping list. Tomte likes to be treated to porridge, especially with a pat of butter on Christmas Eve.

I grew concerned that the Tomte had become a bit too real for Maya. I asked her if we should finish studying about them. "Oh, no! No. No!" So, I asked what could be done to allay her fears. She did not have answers to her pressing questions and that worried her. Would a Tomte harm her grandmother even if the family was nice to it? Could the Tomte's bite be fatal? They did not have porridge, so would some other cereal do? Yes, she *really* needed this information.

I have a dear friend whose husband is one of the world's foremost experts on Scandinavian medieval studies and folklore. I had not anticipated involving him, but Maya was anxious and tends toward an anxiety disorder, as I had learned from her mother. I asked if Maya was willing to write down her questions and I would email them to my friend, who had agreed to pose them to her husband. He treated her concerns very respectfully. He answered: They came on their sleds, not on sleighs. Tomtar rarely bite and there was no known reference to anyone dying. A Tomte knew when a family was being kind. Porridge is what the rural families ate. What kind of cereal did Maya eat regularly? Since she ate Lucky Charms, the house Tomte would be very pleased with that. No need to add butter since that is not how she ate her cereal. Maya reasoned that the mini-marshmallows would be the "extra treat" like the traditional pat of butter. Crisis averted.

She calmly drafted her essay describing Tomtar. It was 1½ pages long and very detailed. She created topic sentences for each new paragraph and indented them. The writing flowed well between paragraphs. Now, Maya's work demonstrated many of the 4th-grade standards – writing a narrative (real or imaginary), using sensory language, and writing a conclusion. The longest paragraph described a Tomte's behavior. It began with a topic sentence and had a logical sequence of ideas. The paragraph contained four complex sentences, a serial list of descriptions, was punctuated correctly (including comma usage), had good details, and ended with a concluding sentence. Maya attempted using expressive vocabulary, although some words were not spelled correctly: gurdian [sic]; extermily [sic] for extremely; and poisoness [sic].

Her first draft is as follows:

> The behavior of the Tomte is either nice or evil. If you give the Tomte porage [sic] with butter then he will keep his job as your gurdian [sic] but if you wrong the Tomte bad things will happen. When the Tomte has been wronged or offended, it will sit on your head and give you nightmares, steal your sausages, tangle your hair, cause mischif [sic], etc. If the Tomte is extermily [sic] angry then it can give you poisoness [sic] bites or even quit his job as gurdian [sic] of your farm and leave.

## Creative Writing

As we resumed in January, I heard that the "house Tomte" had behaved and that Maya was not ready to be done with Tomtar. I had prepared for this possibility. Had Maya ever written a story? No, she had not. I showed her a brief video of a local children's author, Mac Barnett, who talked about preparing to write a story (www.ted.com/talks/mac_barnett_why_a_good_book_is_a_secret_door?language=en).

As she was watching, Maya shouted, "Wait! Wait! I've met him!" When the video was over, she told me that he had come to her school when she was in the 3rd grade and as a result, Maya "had even checked out a couple of his picture books from the library."

I shared the differences between fiction and nonfiction. Did she have an idea for a story? Yes! She set up a storyboard with three sections "about him", "no respect", and "oscar takes action" to plan her work and had already named the Tomte, Oscar. She rapidly filled in details about what he looked like, his jobs on the farm, why he liked being on the farm, and how long he had lived there.

"Sorry. This is taking a **long** time. I'm writing a lot! Can I leave the part about 'Oscar takes action' as a surprise?"

"Do you know what you are going to write about?"

"Definitely!"

"Okay, then", was my response. I reminded her about punctuating contractions and she nodded and I briefly reviewed using quotations marks in dialogue.

"I was going to do that **already**", she chided me.

Maya began writing with great concentration. After 14 minutes I asked, "Still writing?"

"Yes. I'm sorry I'm taking so long. It's a whole page", she said proudly.

"Does that feel good?" She answered with a broad smile and a nod.

After a few more minutes I asked, "Need a spelling break?" No. She wanted to continue writing.

"Now I'm writing about what the cows are feeling, what happened to the farm, and what happened to Oscar." She wrote almost tirelessly over many more sessions.

She would screenshare and read aloud to me at the end of every session. I was impressed by her characterizations, the emotions in her dialogue, and the flow in her story.

"Do you want to edit as you go?"

"No. Keep writing!" At times she would chortle aloud, enjoying the humor in her story. (She had named all the farmer's cows after her friends and one got turned into beef stew!)

"It's even longer than my Cinderella work! It's almost 7 pages! I have **never** written this much!"

"I'm proud of you, Maya", I told her and asked, "More importantly, are you proud of yourself?"

"Yes", she answered quietly.

Final edits were needed but those did not diminish the quality of her work. Now, she was able to quickly locate most of her errors when directed to a specific sentence or section.

I asked if she would have been able to read her work and independently find the errors. She answered that she could not. "Why not?" I asked.

"Because I just don't see them."

I asked if I could share her story with her mother. She did NOT want me to do that.

"Why not, Maya? It is really good work." No answer, just a shrug. I made an intuitive guess. "If I typed it up, could I share it?" She agreed. It seemed she still felt the burden of having "messy" handwriting. Here is an excerpt from the start of her story:

> A long time ago, a Tomte lived in an isolated farm in Sweden. The Tomte was 3 ft. tall with a long white beard and a long hat that drags on the floor. The Tomte's name was Oscar. Oscar has worked on the farm for hundreds of years and he loves [sic] it here. There are so many animals to play with and the porridge was great. Oscar loved his job but felt he was no longer respected.

This appeared to be a breakthrough moment in developing her writing skills because she enjoyed the writing process, had written more than ever before, and demonstrated a specific writing talent. Interestingly, she told me that she had never been asked to write a story before.

## Summary

I had learned that Maya had an affinity and ability for creative writing. She enjoyed it and likely, this skill could be developed further. She was successful and enjoyed writing a sustained piece. Writing dialogue came very naturally and, perhaps, all the movies she had watched contributed to that. More work was needed on punctuating prepositional phrases and on lessening the number of run-on sentences. Unfortunately, Maya was not **reading** the required book for English; nor was anyone aware that she was not comprehending it.

Notetaking to guide her writing had been very productive. By writing to compare the versions of Cinderella and her Tomte story, Maya had demonstrated writing to 4th-grade standards in her work with me. However, she was not generalizing her skills into her school work, as she felt her teachers did not value or grade her actual writing skills. I wondered how to ensure that her newly acquired skills could be generalized. The parents requested a change in resource specialist teacher, beginning in January. This request was flatly denied but would be "revisited for Maya's 8th-grade year." Additionally, Maya's father discovered that educational therapy payments could be reimbursed using his workplace Flexible Spending Account (FSA).

## Reference

Barnett, M. (2014, June). *TED* [Video]. www.ted.com/talks/mac_barnett_why_a_good_book_is_a_secret_door?language=en

# 6 Superheroes and Greek Gods and Goddesses

## February–April

Since Maya was not reading her required English text with any comprehension, she needed direct instruction in effective techniques to better understand and recall what she read. Maya was excited about superheroes and many new movies featuring them were being produced. She regarded Stan Lee as an icon in the genre and read a several-page-long biography that I had created for her. She also read about Wonder Woman, Dr. Strange, and The Black Panther using articles from ReadWorks. Again, I created and inserted open-ended questions for the multiple-choice ones. Maya had never heard of or utilized the reading comprehension strategy of reading the questions first, to focus one's reading. This approach was helpful and my notes state that "she was able to track essential ideas better" using this method. Now, she could answer questions, in writing, without confusing details for essential ideas. However, she could not formulate any questions for **me** to answer. I requested she ask me questions beyond "Yes or No" ones. This is a much harder skill, as it requires determining the main ideas **and** taking a more active role in understanding the material. Obviously, I moved too quickly by assuming she could now formulate questions based on her recognition of key ideas. Instead of merely recalling information, one must interact with the material by analyzing and thinking critically about it. I would revisit this activity later. But now, notetaking by reading the questions first continued to be an effective way to organize and generate greater written output such as this example:

> In history, Wonder Woman had been around since 1941. She was an Amazon Warrior named Princess Diana. Wonder Woman debuted in All Star Comics and then later got her own comics. For a time [sic]she was a secretary for the Justice League and never got to participate in any of the action. In 1977, a Wonder Woman's series started on ABC

television. Then, Wonder Woman got a movie that was rated in the top ten films of 2017.

Some differences about Wonder Woman are she is sassy, female, and was only a secretary. Her comics were mostly aimed for girls. Her comics were more humerous [sic] and funny than most other comics. Wonder Woman starred on the cover of Ms. Magazine Wonder Woman had many differences from other super heross [sic].

Maya still enjoyed the spelling drills. She spelled words at the 5th-grade level correctly. Now, I required her to use specific words in complete sentences. She balked at this, but she was generally successful. When I directed her to use three of the spelling words (each) in a sentence, she asked, "If I can use all three words in *one* sentence, can I write only one?"

"Sure, if it is a good sentence." Challenge accepted and her sentence was correct.

However, writing a summary and stating the main idea still proved to be a struggle. Maya tended to rely on her ability to recall information and simply "retell" what she gleaned from the article. I observed that she was struggling with her focus and attention again.

"Maya, are you still taking the Ritalin?" I asked.

"No. I quit. It was making me feel anxious."

I discussed with Maya how I observed how much better she could focus and recall past learning when medicated.

"I do focus better, but I don't want to feel anxious", was her response.

I said that I did not want her to feel anxious either and would discuss with her mother the need to explore a different medication option. Her mother agreed to request a phone consultation with Maya's doctor who prescribed the ADHD medication. Another medication was provided.

## Greek Gods and Goddesses

In the meanwhile, I hoped to create another ongoing and sustained unit. I searched for a text-like book that she would read, continue taking notes, and explicitly practice summarization skills.

I suggested a related area, Greek gods and goddesses, to Maya. She was intrigued partly because the book I had chosen had "stunning artwork" by award-winning illustrator Christina Balit (School Library Journal Best Books of 2011). The *Treasury of Greek Mythology: Classic Stories of Gods, Goddesses, Heroes and Monsters* (Donna Jo Napoli, National Geographic, Washington D.C., October 2011) was well-regarded. It had won the School Library Journal Best Books of 2011, the Eureka! Silver Honor Books, awarded by the California Reading Association, and is on the Capitol

Choices 2012 list of Noteworthy Titles for Children and Teens. I requested that her mother order her a copy so that we could each be reading from the same text. Scanning this oversized book, with its powerful illustrations and beautiful borders would be difficult and might violate the book's copyrights.

The book highlighted 25 gods and goddesses and I asked Maya to choose several to read about, take notes, and summarize. Later, I would ask her to create a "character study" of each. A character study is a typical assignment in the 3rd and 4th grades as a prerequisite to understanding more challenging texts. Character analysis is necessary to understand how characters are influenced by the book's plot and a character's relationships with others. This was the teacher's intent of assigning the English text, and Maya was missing this practice.

Maya questioned whether people *actually believed* in gods and goddesses and their life events. "Really? Oh, come on! Athena was born out of a forehead?"

After reading the introduction and having a discussion with her, Maya wrote: "Greeks bealive [*sic*] in and created gods so they can answer the questions they don't really understand, to reflect on themselves, and finally to help them understand the complexity of life." She understood key concepts although her tenses varied.

She enjoyed reading about all of the gods and goddesses she had chosen, but was particularly captivated by the myth of Athena and Arachne.

She asked, "How are we going to write about it?"

"We are not going to write about that myth. You are."

Educational therapists have to guard against becoming enmeshed in their student's struggles. The language one uses can be a useful tool and opportunity to clarify one's role. We are sympathetic to the struggle and in a helping role, but one is not going to do the work *for* the student. One remediates but does not create a learning dependency. When Maya used her "little girl voice", she was used to being enabled. Maya needed to believe in her own ability to write.

Maya wrote 11 complex sentences, which included dialogue and expressive vocabulary such as "confident", "representing", "egotistical", "foolish", and "enraged." She had understood that the Greek myths often taught a moral so ended with "don't be so egotistical that you challenge a god."

Maya wrote,

> Arachne was weaving at her loom when an old lady walked up to her and asked,
> 
> "Who taught you how to weave so well?" Arachne being very egotistical said, "I taught myself and I am the best in the land. I'm better than Athena." Athena took off her disguise and enraged said, "How dare you think that you were better than a goddess! Let's have a contest to

see who is better. If I win you will never touch a loom again and if you win I will never weave again." Arachne agreed. She was very confident that she would win – a little too confident. On the day of the contest, Arachne made a tapestry showing the gods and goddesses looking foolish. On the other hand, Athena wove a tapestry representing strength. Athena won and Arachne was very upset – so upset that she decided to take her own life but Athena stopped her and turned her into a spider so that she could still weave. The moral of the story is don't be so egotistical that you will challenge a god.

In summarizing the first god, Helios, she wrote five complete sentences, with only one run-on sentence. However, she included, "Well, it can blind you if you look directly at the sun.", a statement not in the book. Maya was told to not include information outside of the text, as she was prone to relying on her background. Maya complied, as usual.

## Integrating Mechanics While Writing

I *challenged* Maya to not edit after every sentence but to try to incorporate proper mechanics as she wrote. Maya always rose to a direct challenge. In describing Selene, the Moon Goddess, Maya wrote for 17 minutes from her graphic organizer and produced eight relatively complex sentences. She had one error in word tense but she indented the new paragraph, punctuated contractions correctly, comma usage was correct, and all sentences had appropriate capitals and ending punctuation. She was thinking and writing sentence by sentence but not editing after each. Instead, she was incorporating capital letters and punctuations, and though her work was generally correct, it was laborious; it took her about two minutes to write each sentence.

"Maya, does it feel good to write in complete sentences?"

She responded with many vigorous nods.

"I want you to feel this good all the time when you are writing."

Given her greatly improved writing stamina, I wondered if she had changed medications and would check with her mother.

## Creating Character Studies

After summarizing each god or goddess, I asked Maya to describe some aspects of each persona in writing. "Poseidon felt trapped his entire life because he was swallowed by his father. Then, he had to be a solider [sic] in a tedious war for 10 years. But when the war was on a pause, he found joy in the little things like rippling eels, whales, and the ocean."

"Selene's character is shy and sad. She seemed like more of an introvert then [*sic*] an extravert." Maya enjoyed attributing color and sensory details to the gods. "I think Selene is very observational. She would have a high pitched [*sic*] voice and she reminds me of rain."

"Helios looked like a ball of light brightening everyones day [*sic*]."

She created a column graphic organizer so she could describe each god or goddess. She originally included "looks, acts, mood, sound, and color." When I asked if there was anything else she added, "thoughts on humans." This addition was very insightful, as each god/goddess had a unique perspective on and relationship with humans.

For example, she described Eos, the Goddess of the Dawn, as looks: as pink- reminds me of a rose; acts: nice, helpful, useful; mood: peaceful, optimistic; sounds like: has a whispery voice that gets louder into a crescendo; about humans: fell in love with many/ cursed by Zeus so that each died; her last (lover) was turned into a cricket.

Maya could describe each god or goddess, but she could not usually define a specific word, (for example, predictably) although she could use it in a sentence. I wondered whether this was an expressive language weakness or demonstrated a lack of vocabulary. I would continue to note and explore these questions.

Although Maya was writing more, she would ask before nearly every sentence, "Can I say this?"

This underscored her insecurity with writing and that she never understood that written language is just that – one's inner language written down, albeit more formally. Younger writers begin by writing as they speak. Maya had missed this stage. So, struggling with *what* to write became enmeshed with *how* to write.

Despite her uncertainty, she pronounced her writing was "choppy." Her English teacher was instructing the class in using semicolons, so she decided, "I am going to write longer sentences." She changed "Eos is the Dawn Goddess. She opens up the gates of heaven" to "Eos is the Dawn Goddess; she opens up the gates of heaven for her brother Helios." However, she did not supply the comma in the appositive, which she had demonstrated previously. Likely, she was concentrating on using the semicolon correctly.

During this point in her comparison of Greek gods and goddesses, Maya surprised me by announcing that there were many references to Greek gods and goddesses in movies she had watched. I challenged her to write about that new awareness and she eagerly complied with her insights, culminating in an essay that detailed commonalities between such disparate movies as Steven Universe and My Little Pony!

## Using Mad Libs

Because Maya was still confused by parts of speech and played Mad Libs with her friends, I found a free online resource that would create them (www.glowwordbooks.com/kids/madlibs/0). Maya loved this work! I gave her the topic, pizza, in advance, and she created a list of nouns and then a set of verbs she might use. At this point, she only thought of nouns as "things" and could not supply any proper nouns, and knew "action verbs" but not "is, are, was, were, etc." We reviewed this. The directions in the online program helped teach these concepts, too.

> Fill out these questions to generate your own silly mad libs story instantly online! (Hint: a **Verb** is an action. An **adverb** usually ends in "ly" and describes an action (like slowly).
> 
> A **noun** is a person/place/thing. An **adjective** describes a person/place/thing.)

The resulting Pizza Party Mad Lib amused her so much that she asked to take a picture of it with her phone to send to her friends. I prepared Mad Libs for many more sessions, much to Maya's delight as a means to expand her awareness of parts of speech.

Also, because Maya spelled phonetically, as she heard the word, she had never heard nor understood the difference between *then* and *than*. After a short course of practice, Maya readily understood the difference and used them correctly in her writing.

## More Creative Writing

Thinking that she might enjoy another opportunity to engage in creative writing, I suggested she write a dialogue between some of the Greek gods and/or goddesses. Maya wrote an exchange between Helios, the Sun God, and his sisters, Eos and Selene. Although brief, it demonstrated some understanding of each character and hinted at sibling jealousy.

> "Ugh, time to get up already? So early?" said Eos as she rolled out of bed.
> "Calm down, Eos, you're not the one that has to do all the traveling!" Helios said in an angry tone.
> "It's not fair that Selene gets to wake up so late while we have to get up so early!" whined Eos.
> "Hmm jealous aren't we", Selene said with a smirk on her face.
> "Well obviously!" Eos and Helios both shouted.

"This is good", Maya stated.

"That's because you are a very good creative writer. That's become clear to me. Is it clear to you?"

She answered, "Yeah", with no hesitation.

I noticed how apt her word choice was in describing each character's mood in their dialogue. The depth of her vocabulary was emerging more clearly in her writing.

I believed the unit had concluded and was satisfied with her work, so I was surprised when Maya asked, "What about Pan?"

"What about Pan?" I inquired.

"I want to learn about him", was her simple answer.

"We can do that."

## Self-directed Learning

Once again, Maya showed initiative and a "spark" of self-directed learning. Pan was not in our book, being a lesser god, but I happily found information for our next session.

She read independently and asked about the meanings of *depicted* and *unsightly*. Despite reading fluently, I stopped her after each section and asked for the main idea or a question about an essential detail. She recalled little. I suggested Maya write "little notes" for each section. The "little notes" were mini-summaries which created better understanding. She wrote,

> Pan, God of the Wild, ruled over nature, wooded areas, and pasture lands. He was depicted with horns and an unsightly face. He was often accompanied by wood nymphs and other forest creatures. Pan had many powers, he could teleport, run for a while, impervious to injery [*sic*], and could turn things into objects. Pan made the musical instrument, the pan flute. The word panic was given to us by Pan. In the 1800s [*sic*] Pan was the central figure of many festivals.

"Is Pan related to Peter Pan?" was her question.

"I don't know, Maya. They could be since both are mischievous" was my answer. Maya was making interesting connections again. I was impressed at her word choices and that she readily incorporated new words such as *depicted* and *impervious* correctly.

Maya stated that now she wanted to read about Iris, a Messenger Goddess, since she was depicted with a rainbow. I found new content and challenged her to read so that she could create questions for me to answer.

Maya was able to write the following:

1) How was Iris depicted?
2) Who was the better messenger, Iris or Hermes?
3) Who were Iris' parents?

Two were simply recall questions but she was able to create them and we had a lively debate over the second one, "Who was the better messenger?" She said Hermes because he had more territory to cover. I said Iris because, being a woman, she had to work harder to have her efforts appreciated.

Then, she surprised me by asking if we could study one more god, Nyx. "Of course!" was my response. Maya wanted to learn more since she had recently watched a short action movie about this character. Then, she added even more unexpected information – she had begun researching Nyx *on her own*. In her last two written summaries of Iris and Nyx, Maya was now able to self-review, find her mistakes and correct them. These were notable improvements so I said to her,

"You are writing well now." I wondered how much carryover (transference) was seen in her school work. "Are you writing in complete sentences at school?"

"Sometimes. Not really. Not much", was her honest response. "They just don't care", was the refrain. Sadly, she said none of her work was returned with any feedback or comments.

## Writing a Persuasive Essay: Crystals

In our regular conversation, I told her mother I wanted to move Maya into a nonfiction area of study. She informed me that a new fascination had taken hold; Maya was persuaded by the possibility that crystals could heal. Maya had begun collecting them and suggested crystals as a topic for writing. Rather than discourage the latest interest, I chose to embrace Maya's choice as a natural vehicle to practice reading nonfiction texts. I would teach her an annotated notetaking method to propel her beyond the bullet points system she had been using thus far.

Together we chose a book with lots of colored pictures (Frasier, Karen. *Crystals for Beginners: The Guide to Get Started with the Healing Power of Crystals*. Berkeley, CA, Althea Press, 2017). The book was divided into two sections: an overview about crystals and the second part featured each crystal's purported powers for healing. I also contributed published articles describing double-blind studies evaluating whether using crystals actually seemed to heal. I had her read one of these during one of our early sessions on this topic, creating an opening for a discussion of the placebo effect. She wrote the following:

- no scientific evidence
- keep an open mind [be]cause people swear by them
- vairity [sic] and what they do

Maya read the first chapter very carefully using the new notetaking method. She was directed to annotate, in her book, using color. *New words* would be marked in blue; *important ideas* would be marked in pink; *key details* would be marked in green. Maya chose the colors for each. This was an opportunity to revisit determining key points and a reminder to not skip over unknown words, as subjects in middle-school texts often had topic-specific vocabulary. A bit later, I suggested she add another color for her probing questions; she chose yellow. Maya did not want to annotate her book by using highlighter pens. "It'd ruin it." However, I had anticipated this possibility and had asked her mother to purchase small reels of highlighter tape which come in different colors and can be removed from a text after use (ReallyGoodStuff.com) and small "sticky notes" in various colors. I usually provide and demonstrate all of these products along with the practice of creating "margin notes", allowing the student to experiment with each and finally choose the material that works best (E-texts can be highlighted online, too.). Maya chose to use colored "sticky notes", which she combined with the usual Four Square graphic organizer.

## Essay Preparation

In getting ready to write her essay, Maya noted that one of her quadrants had a mixture of content so she asked, "These ideas don't all belong together. What should I do?"

"It's good you noticed that. What should you do?" (That meant she was reading and taking notes with good comprehension.)

"Well, I could separate this into two sections."

"That sounds like a good plan. What would each of these sections be?"

"Different paragraphs."

"What do paragraphs do?"

"They organize for the reader."

"Maya, who is the reader?"

"Well, right now, it's you and me. And, I kinda need to go out of order in the bullets in this one section."

"If that's what makes sense, fine. We don't always list everything in the correct order when we take notes", was my response.

"I could write a paragraph without looking at my notes", Maya claimed.

"Really? You're on! And since we are nearing the end of our session, you will have to wait to do that until next time – and without your notes."

"What have I done to myself?" wailed Maya.

Since several days had intervened, I reminded her of her boastful claim and asked her to begin a summary paragraph of any aspect of the crystals book's introduction that she chose. Of course, the task was much harder than she had anticipated.

Finally, she said, "It's a mess. I can't do it."

"Do you think it was the time delay that made it so hard?"

"Maybe. Probably not. I guess notes help you remember stuff", Maya conceded as she reached for her notes.

Using her notes, Maya produced a 3½ page essay describing crystals, common beliefs about them, associated myths, the unique powers associated with specific crystals, and "doubts and skepticism" about their efficacy as agents of healing. She also attempted a complete concluding paragraph which had appropriate transition words such as *first, then, next,* and *finally*.

Following is the first draft of her final section of the essay:

> Some people say that its [*sic*] all in your head and crystals can't actually heal. There is very little evidence showing that a crystal can heal. The Placebo Effect is when you are given something fake and beilive [*sic*] it's real so you think it will benifit [*sic*] you. Belief in this object maybe enough to change the course of a person's physical illness. There was an experiment involving the Placebo Effect and crystals. In this experiment, half of the people were given crystals and the other half was [*sic*] given fake plastic crystals. Both of the groups said they felt the positive energy of the crystals. That is an example of the Placebo Effect. Some people think that expensive crystals are the most powerful, but it doesn't matter how much you spend. What matters is how it affects your energy. Some may say that crystals don't have their own vibration and they can't balance [sic] your energy or heal you. Others may say that crystals can't balance [sic] out your spiritual energy.

## Saliency Determination

Over the next few weeks, she studied the purported properties of specific crystals. Of the 35 crystals detailed in the book, she chose four to study in detail. They were some of her favorites – rose quartz, amethyst, moonstone, and malachite. Each crystal's description was very thorough, which necessitated her deciding on the key elements to include. Saliency determination is the ability to determine what is important. Determining saliency enables the learner to allocate sufficient attentional resources where needed. It is a difficult skill for many students. For Maya, it was critical to learn to establish saliency by evaluating whether something was a "key idea" or an extraneous detail. This was related to her long-standing issue with ascertaining the main idea. Apparently, she had never been instructed about determining saliency when taking notes. I stated that the mind cannot pay attention to everything equally. The mind needs to know what is important in order to focus one's attention. As focal maintenance was often an issue for Maya, determining saliency was an important skill to practice. I explained why highlighting everything in a passage is **not** helpful to understanding the content and does not aid in recall.

"Wait! Wait! I get to pick? I can leave some stuff out? Cool!" was her enthusiastic comment.

The book detailed six different "crystal lattice patterns" with each crystal having a hexagonal, isometric, monoclinic, orthorhombic, tetragonal, or triclinic interior structure. It was critical for her to determine if this was salient information or not, given her proclivity for "skipping over" unfamiliar words or parts of a text and for misconstruing details for the main idea. After some deliberation, Maya reasoned that the interior patterns of each crystal were not germane to discussing its healing properties.

Her resulting graphic organizer listed the country of origin, the stone's color, what the stone "helps with", whether it was an "amplifier" or an "absorber", and the ideal location on the body to wear it or place it. The resulting three-page essay was written clearly (albeit a bit formulaic in sentence construction), had a paragraph describing each crystal accurately, used commas appropriately, and concluded with a paragraph that added in one sentence of summative information, "Many of my favorite crystals come from Brazil." The first draft of two paragraphs is as follows:

> Moonstone originates from Austria, Brazil, India, and Sri Lanka. [The text capitalized each crystal.] There are three different colors Moonstone can be. Moonstone can be black, white, or peach. A Moonstone's energy is an amplifier. Moonstone works well with Rose Quartz and Amethyst. Moonstone can be worn as a necklace or it can be placed near the third eye or crown chakra.
>
> Malachite originates from the Congo, the Middle East, Russia, and Zambia. Malachite is green. Malachite is a protective crystal so, instead of amplifying it absorbs energy. Malachite helps with absorbing negative energy, protecting against accidents, and relieving [*sic*] fears associated with air travel. Malachite works well with Lapis Lazuli. It can be placed on a carron bag during air travel or near the heart chakra.

## Summary

I had learned that reading, notetaking, and writing were becoming well-linked for Maya. Practice with expository texts was beneficial in recognizing key ideas, determining saliency, and summarizing. She was now reading for meaning. Specific techniques to improve her reading comprehension were helpful. Similarly, Maya asked for definitions of unfamiliar words instead of merely skipping over them, as in the past. Although there were still some run-on sentences, her use of commas was much improved, including punctuating appositives correctly. Maya's improvement in her writing skills, stamina, and attention had noticeably increased with the new medication. It appeared that, as her writing prowess improved, so did the vocabulary she used in her work. I would need to verify this hypothesis.

Addressed were numerous details about her writing, including plurals and possessives, as well as words she had confused. This "reminding" or "reteaching" seemed to be helpful to her editing process and produced a better finished product.

Maya was engaged in connecting our work to her background knowledge and coming up with some unique insights. Self-directed learning had emerged. She enjoyed using the "colored sticky notes" to annotate articles and her text. "I'm really good at annotation", was Maya's announcement. Annotation helped her recall information, organize, decide what information was salient, and prepare to write. Importantly, the culminating paragraph required **no edits** beyond what she corrected, **by herself**, in rereading it. I theorized that she could not "see her mistakes" before because Maya did not really know correct writing mechanics. Would her improved writing and self-editing skills transfer to her school work?

Lastly, the family informed me that the discussions between the district and the family lawyer had "stalled out." I would be informed, in advance, of the trial dates and I should endeavor to make myself available and ready to serve as a witness.

## Reference

Glow Word Books. www.glowwordbooks.com/kids/madlibs/0/

# 7 The Final Three Months

## May–August

### Trial Preparation

The family's lawyer recommended the parents observe what was happening in the (virtual) Resource class as a part of the preparation for the upcoming trial. They were assured that watching was legal and did not require any notification to the teacher or school. Her mother and father each took a turn observing and taking time-annotated notes over the course of ten consecutive school days. They were shocked by what they observed. Maya's mother sent me a daily copy of her notes, I believed not so much as a "need to know", but as a way to vent her frustrations and dismay.

Maya was apparently so inured to not having her camera on, not having to focus, and to not responding that it did not matter that a parent was sitting behind her. She continued on, as she had much of the semester. Maya played video games on her phone, texted friends, or watched cartoons on her iPad during the class time. Apparently, though, she was listening for certain cues. Because, when her teacher announced that she would be sharing the **answers** to the comprehension questions posed by Maya's English teacher, Maya would stop whatever activity she was engaged in and take a screenshot. Then, she would go to her English class portal and enter in the correct answers, disregarding expected writing conventions. When asked by her mother, the English teacher said that Maya was earning an A- for her reading comprehension work. Why not an A, since all the answers were correct, I wondered? I had chosen to read the book along with Maya so that I could help her comprehend it. From my questioning, it was clear that she was **not** tracking **any** of the key developments in the book, *The True Confessions of Charlotte Doyle* by Avi. Now I understood. Why should she? All of the comprehension work was being done *for her* (and for others in the Resource program). I felt heartsick about the message this sent to Maya and the others in her support class.

DOI: 10.4324/9781003284741-7

## Further Shocking Discoveries

Maya was required to prepare another research paper for her science class. Whereas, she had felt panicked by the assignment before, her attitude was considerably more relaxed this time. Was it because she had greater confidence in her ability to organize and write? I asked if she wanted to use some of our session time to work on it.

"No, I've got it", was her breezy answer. This was very uncharacteristic of her usual worries about her writing. So, I probed a bit more.

"How are you organizing the paragraphs, Maya?"

"Just like you taught me. Four squares and bullet points."

I wanted to feel relieved but something seemed off. "Can I see your work so far?"

"Sure", was her easy reply. She screenshared with me, got into her school portal, and located her in-progress science paper.

"Maya, I see you have written a lot so far. Good. When is it due?"

"In two days", was her unnaturally relaxed answer.

I began to read some of it. "I see lots of editing notations. Some of this sounds like your work – like the way you write, but some of it doesn't." Some parts were written with much more formal sentence structures than Maya had mastered yet.

She replied with a casual glance at her work, "Yes. I write some stuff. Then, either my English teacher or Resource teacher fix it. See – my Resource teacher changed all the order of my paragraphs."

I was shocked. "Then what happens?" I asked.

"They fix it and tell me to accept all the changes and submit it as my work."

I tried very hard to not to convey any reaction although I was horrified. Were they colluding to do her work for her? Did they think that was appropriate? What did Maya understand by these actions? That she could not write? How could the district insist that she no longer needed special education services if she was so incapable that work was being done for her? I texted her mother and asked for a phone conference with her parents. Her mother thought I must have misunderstood, but said she would ask Maya in a very casual manner so Maya would not suspect anything might be wrong. She came away shaken, too, as Maya confirmed this is how she was writing longer assignments now. Someone "fixed her work" and she just accepted all the changes.

Maya's mother was able to look back at other English assignments and see that these massive edits had been occurring with regularity. The family set up a strategy meeting with the lawyer and included me. The lawyer asked Maya's mother to make copies of these assignments from the school portal but stated, "We really don't need them. We have plenty of ammunition and evidence."

For my part, I was asked to prepare a one-page document about her current level of writing and executive functioning skills. The district personnel had said, in our last IEP meeting, that a goal for Maya's executive functioning would be entertained. The lawyer asked that I create a document which included goals that would be submitted to the district and the court. In it, I shared my views about what was occurring. (Only the name has been changed on this document.)

*Area of Educational Need: Written Language*

As of April 28, 2021, Maya is performing substantially differently in the 1:1 educational therapy sessions versus in her school setting. The primary difference is her sense of accountability. Will she be held accountable for her work? Is she expected to comprehend and recall the information in assigned texts and write at grade-level expectations? Or will copious accommodations that modify grade-level expectations be given, including the sharing of answer keys, editing her writing such that she can simply "accept" the changes without needing to do any analysis or learning? Will written work be accepted that has limited (or no) capitalization and punctuation and utilizes incomplete or run-on sentences?

In both settings she continues to struggle with recalling information she has read, summarizing it, making predictions, and answering inferential questions in writing. At school, Maya does not often write in complex sentences that evidence the standards of written English. In the 1:1 setting, she can now plan, write, use capitalization and ending punctuation, and edit her own work without prompting. For this to become habitual and integrated into her daily work, Maya's school must expect the same and consider it in grading her work.

**Recommended Goal:** Given multiple-paged text, at a grade appropriate Lexile Level of 925–1185, Maya will write **independently,** demonstrating the standard conventions of written English by:

a) summarizing the text
b) answering 4/5 inferential comprehension questions correctly
c) writing what newly introduced vocabulary means in her own words at 85% accuracy
d) choosing a graphic organizer 100% of the time
e) using that graphic organizer to write a well-constructed essay consisting of an introductory paragraph, 3 supportive paragraphs, and a concluding paragraph

This essay will be scored by the online scoring for the WIAT-4 "Essay Composition" subtest with Maya scoring at the end of the 6th-grade level, or higher.

*Area of Educational Need: Organization/Study Skills*

Maya demonstrates some existing strengths in her executive function skills. In the 1:1 setting, she is always punctual, has the required materials safeguarded, organized and ready. To demonstrate these same qualities at school, Maya will **independently**:

a) use and fill-in a weekly homework planner 90% of the time
b) be able to state when each homework assignment is due 100% of the time
c) gauge and track her progress toward completion of larger projects or long-term assignments 80% of the time
d) turn in each assignment, on time and without adult reminders, 85% of the time over the course of a month

Respectfully Submitted:
Marion Marshall, MS, Board Certified Educational Therapist #10176,
Emerita Professor Holy Names University

## Arbitration Hearing

A week-long arbitration hearing was scheduled to begin. I was on "stand-by" to be called to testify, if needed. All of us were anxious. After two days, I received a text from the family's lawyer stating, "I don't think you will be needed. The judge has reviewed your recorded and very consistent statements at the IEP meetings." I was told that I would not be a party to any of the specific details about any agreements reached, but was told I would hear something at the conclusion. Maya's mother texted me regularly stating that "things were very tense." On the fifth day, I received a phone message from the family's lawyer saying, "The best possible outcomes were achieved. Very satisfying end to this long-standing school situation." Later, I was told, "I can't go into any details but expect to be employed by the family for all of next year, too."

*Regarding Special Education Law Challenges*

Special Education lawsuits can be expensive for a school district in California, which is why it was so puzzling that the district adamantly refused

Maya an IEP and one period of Resource support per day. The school already employed an RS supporting students in Maya's grade with writing issues. No additional personnel were needed. If a district loses the court case, it is often required to repay the parents for their attorney fees and for any additional legal counsel. And this does not take into account the time already spent on meetings for this case or for legal counsel the district hired. Also, a judge may order a district to pay for additional nonschool services, which is what resulted when the RS stated I was to "catch Maya up", as it was not her job. Maya had her IEP reinstated until the next triennial review and, apparently, the judge ordered the school district to pay the family retroactively for my fees from August 2020 to the court date and through the next full year (including summers.)

### *WIAT III Assessment by the District*

The district had waited until the last week of school to reassess Maya's writing. This was a bit of strategic gamesmanship because, in California, if a request to assess comes in the final two weeks of a school year, the district legally has until 30 days into the next school year to hold the IEP meeting to discuss the results [Cal. Ed. Code Sec. 56344 (a)]. Also, the "permission to assess" parental document was flawed. The WIAT III was not listed as the assessment instrument, as previously agreed upon. The reason given was that the resource specialist stated she did not know how to give it. That was likely true, as many resource specialists are only trained to give the WJ IV Tests of Achievement. However, the family held firm and the school district found a Program Specialist, in their employ, to give the writing subtests: "Sentence Composition", "Essay Composition", and "Spelling."

Maya went to school in June to take the test. She said it was "eerie" going to school since no other students were present. Walking the empty halls was "creepy" and maybe not the ideal setup for being assessed, but Maya told her mother that she "wrote a lot – like a whole page with capitals and periods", she said proudly. Then, her mother asked her what she wrote about.

"I forget", said Maya nonchalantly. I hoped it was a representative sample of her writing and demonstrated her progress. Given her current skills when working with me, I "guestimated" that she might score in the low-average range for her age (or about the end of 4th grade/beginning of the 5th-grade level) on the essay portion of the assessment. However, we would have to wait because, although pressed by the family, the school district restated that the results would not be shared until the beginning of Maya's 8th-grade school year.

As the new school year approached, Maya's family received the assessment report. I have recreated the scoring printout using the information given to her parents for use in this book. (The name and school were omitted.)

- According to the district's report, Maya scored at the 63rd percentile rank for *Spelling*, as she correctly spelled 39 out of the 50 words given to her.
- The Sentence Composition contains two subtests – *Sentence Combining* and *Sentence Building*. On the *Sentence Combining* task, the student is asked to combine two or three short sentences into one longer sentence. Maya correctly combined sentences at the 70th percentile rank. Notably, the sentences were **already** created for her. On the *Sentence Building* subtest, the student is asked to write one sentence using a specific "target word." Maya correctly created sentences resulting in a score in the 37th percentile rank and the report noted that on three of the seven items, she did not use ending punctuation. For Maya, sentence creation was much more challenging than combining existing sentences.
- On the *Essay Composition* subtest, the student creates an essay within a ten-minute time limit. Maya wrote an essay that contained an introduction, thesis, and a conclusion. She also correctly included three reasons for her preferred game. The district examiner scored her work at the 75th percentile rank.

The summary stated that Maya's scores, on all of the subtests administered, "suggested" her academic skills related to writing were within the average

*Table 7.1* WIAT III Results

| WIAT III | Standard Score | Percentile (%) | Qualitative Description |
|---|---|---|---|
| **Written Expression** | 109 | 73 | Average |
| Spelling | 105 | 63 | Average |
| Sentence Composition | | | |
| -Sentence Combining | 108 | 70 | |
| -Sentence Building | 95 | 37 | |
| Essay Composition | | | |
| -Word Count | 124 | 95 | Above average |
| -Theme Development and Text Organization | 105 | 63 | Average |
| *Supplemental Subtest:* Essay Composition: Grammar and Mechanics | 110 | 75 | Average |

range or above those of her same-age peers. It is interesting to note that, on the table provided by the district, the apparent discrepancy between her skills on the *Sentence Combining* and *Sentence Building* subtests was not discussed nor labeled in the Qualitative Descriptions.

## Why Had Maya Scored So Well?

Upon receiving this report, Maya's parents were stunned. They shared the report and asked how were these scores possible? I explained that Maya had made real progress. Then, I explained that her spelling, in isolation, had always been a strength. Her ability to write syntactically correct sentences was never in doubt. Her single low score, at the 37th percentile range, seemed plausible because, although she scored in the low-average range, it was noted that she did not use ending punctuation more than half of the time. That seemed realistic, too. What did **not seem** accurate was that her *Essay Composition* score was at the 12th-grade level, as stated in an email to her parents, nor did her score at the 63rd percentile rank on that measure.

I reminded her parents that scoring the essay was very difficult, required a serious study of the manual, practice with the sample tests supplied, and was **very** prone to an inflated score due to the examiner's subjective judgment. That is why I had requested the WIAT 4, as it was now scored by a computer algorithm. I reminded them that they could request a copy of Maya's protocol, a copy of her actual written essay. I would rescore it through the software of the WIAT 4, since I knew the writing prompt was still the same. (That seemed very unfortunate to me that the prompt had not been changed in the latest edition. How many years in a row can students be asked to write about "their favorite game"?)

I suggested they check with their lawyer, but recalled that we had asked to receive a copy of the WIAT III protocol for this exact purpose, as a safeguard. I also knew that a parent's request to have a copy of the protocol had been legally addressed. In 1997, it was determined **not** to be a violation of any copyright laws. "A parent's right to 'inspect and review' education records includes test protocols and answer sheets." FERPA does not create an exception for "copyrighted materials" (www.fetaweb.com/04/ferpa.rooker.ltr.protocols.htm). That right was litigated further in 2005 in California with the same result. A District Court decision, *Newport-Mesa Unified Sch. Dist. v. State of California Dept. of Educ*, "held that providing parents with a copy of test protocols is not a violation of the copyright law, and that parents are permitted such access under the 'fair use' provision of the copyright law" (www.wrightslaw.com/law/caselaw/05/2005.CA.dist.court.newport-mesa.test.protocols.pdf).

Maya's family lawyer agreed and urged them to formally request a copy of the WIAT III "Essay Composition" to be supplied **before** the scheduled IEP meeting in August 2020. The district spokesperson agreed. However, in a stunning turn of events, Maya's mother was informed, just days before our scheduled meeting, that the district had "lost" the test records. She urged the district to search for them. However, they were "not found" and she was told that the Program Specialist who had given Maya the test had "left the district."

This situation seemed wholly unbelievable to me. Districts are legally bound to hold student records and must take extra care to ensure the safety of records of students receiving special education services. Legally, districts must maintain records for three years after the student leaves the district. So, if a student graduates from a public high school, the records must be held until they are 20–21 years old (depending on their age at graduation). In light of COVID-19 and the many IEP meetings being held virtually, the California Department of Education, issued a statement in November 2020, encouraging "local educational agencies (LEAs) to review their current educational record maintenance practices to ensure students' records, including those records of students with disabilities, are secure, up-to-date and accessible" www.cde.ca.gov/sp/se/lr/om111020.asp 11/20.

## One Year Later – Neuropsychology Reassessment

Despite the "loss" of documentation, the district stated they would use the WIAT III test results as their baseline measure. Maya's parents strenuously objected, fearing these assessment results would fuel yet another assault on Maya's eligibility for special education services. I said I could retest her, but immediately withdrew that idea, as it would be seen as a conflict of interest. Maya's mother agreed stating, "And also not a good idea, Marion, because we know she writes for you!" Then, I suggested contacting the neuropsychologist who had assessed her before. Exactly one year had passed, so she could readminister the TOWL-4, the results would be valid, and we would have a year-to-year direct comparison by an unbiased assessor.

Maya's family was very fortunate in the timing of their request, as the neuropsychologist had a last-minute cancellation, otherwise she was booked until January 2021. The neuropsychologist readministered the TOWL-4 and added the Feifer Assessment of Writing to gain additional insights. The results were interesting. Maya's dysgraphia was evidenced by her 6th percentile rank score on the "Alphabet Tracing Fluency" subtest. She scored well on the "Homophone Spelling" subtest (77th percentile rank) "when given options" as is the subtest's format. She had been working on learning the differences between homophones spellings and meanings in our sessions.

Maya scored less well on the "Isolated Spelling" subtest (19th percentile rank) and also at the 19th percentile rank on the "Expository Writing" subtest. The examiner noted Maya had tried "to use organizing words such as 'first...' followed by 'then...', but without much elaboration." Maya scored very well on TOWL-4, as she likely benefitted from having a picture prompt and the opportunity to describe a dramatic scene that could include dialogue. The neuropsychologist wrote, "Overall, Maya has made remarkable progress in writing. She wrote much more freely and produced a greater quantity in 2021 compared to 2020."

According to the neuropsychologist's assessment report, Maya now scored at the following percentile ranks: "Contextual Conventions" 25th percentile (previously the 9th); "Story Composition" 84th (previously the 9th); and "Overall Spontaneous Writing Index" at the 61st percentile (previously the 7th). She concluded her report stating, "Clearly, Maya has benefited greatly from direct educational therapy remediation regarding her writing challenges."

When these results were sent to Maya's parents, her mother was despondent thinking that the district would reassert the issue of eligibility. Maya and I had worked together for a full year now and she had made observable progress since the district's WIAT III assessment. I said, "This is the only time I can recall feeling like I should apologize to parents for the fact that their child had made significant gains!" I added that I had suspected Maya would now score within the average range with only vestiges of her written language disorder still evident. Wisely, her father counseled, "We have to remember that this is **exactly** what we had hoped – for Maya to become a better writer."

Upon reading the neuropsychologist assessment report, the family lawyer was full of praise for Maya's progress and urged calm stating, "You have a court order. The district cannot take away her eligibility for special education services, despite her strong gains." Later, I thought to ask if Maya was medicated during her appointment with the neuropsychologist. Her mother said she had not been, since Maya had not been medicated during her assessment one year prior.

## Summer Work – Executive Functioning

To prepare for summer work, I decided to do some investigation and possible instruction on her executive functioning skills and I started thinking about what books might intrigue her enough to read them. Maya was very interested in taking the questionnaire about her executive functioning skills. She claimed she had never heard the term, which surprised me, as I thought most middle school resource specialists would have done instruction in this area.

"No? Then, study skills?" I asked.

"Oh, that! Yes, we have to write stuff down in our planner."

"Why, Maya?"

"I don't know. We just copy down from the board."

To fully engage in the work, Maya had always needed a clear explanation for *why* I gave her a specific task. So, I explained that executive functioning skills were more than writing assignments down in a planner. I would ask her to rate herself across many domains, using the Dawson and Guare book (Dawson, P., & Guare, R. (2018). *Executive Skills in Children and Adolescents, Third Edition: A Practical Guide to Assessment and Intervention.* The Guilford Press.) Then, I could compile and analyze her responses and we would discuss the results. (This book gives permission for a "qualified purchaser" to copy and use the materials with students.)

Maya willingly participated in the self-rating and I tallied the results. Listed in order, her strengths were Flexibility, Working Memory, Response Inhibition, and Time Management (primarily that she was aware of time passing). Her relative weaknesses were Metacognition, Stress Tolerance, and Task Initiation. Maya's weaknesses were Organization, Sustained Attention, Goal Persistence, and Planning. Once again, Maya demonstrated a good understanding of herself, which is not wholly typical of 13-year-olds, especially those with ADHD.

Nearly one year prior, on the neuropsychologist's Behavior Rating (Inventory of Executive Functioning 2nd Edition (BRIEF-2)), Maya's self-reported rating listed several areas in the "clinically significant" (deficit) range. They were Inhibition, Self-Monitoring, Task Completion, Working Memory, and Planning/Organization. Although she still rated low in many of the domains, she now felt that her working memory was improved. Was that due to the fact that I had purposefully and carefully increased her workload incrementally so that she felt more capable? Was that due to the fact that, when medicated, she *could* do the work more independently? Or, was that perception simply due to the fact that the two different instruments asked different questions?

## Examining Her Strengths

Maya was very intrigued when I shared the results. I carefully explained what each term meant. She knew what "flexibility" meant and said she did not "get all stressed out when plans had to be changed." She agreed that she always knew what time it was and was "never late for anything!" We discussed how that was in conflict with initiating tasks, goal persistence, and planning.

"Yes, I always wait until the last minute to get started on a report or big project."

"Did that cause you stress?" I asked.

"Oh, yeah."

Like many other students receiving special education services, Maya had only heard about her deficit areas. "I'm a big bunch of faults", she whispered sadly. So, she was captivated by the thought that she had *any* strengths. "Tell me about my strengths again", Maya requested. As I reiterated them, I asked her to contribute examples of them, as I had in my explanations to her. She was smiling when we concluded our discussion and asked, "Can I tell my mom about them?" However, it was unclear whether Maya actually wanted to do anything about her long-standing habit of procrastination. I wondered whether summer work would afford opportunities for practicing time management techniques given that school was out and I was managing her workload.

## Summer Work – Reading Novels

Maya was not interested in reading novels. I had requested her mother to join us for part of a session so we could discuss summer work. Maya complained about having to do *any* summer work and argued that she did not want to read books. "I read all the time!" she claimed.

"You do?" asked her mother.

"What do you read, Maya?" I asked.

"I look stuff up and read it on the internet", was her reply.

I told her I would look for books that would interest her – not like *Charlotte Doyle*.

She did not like graphic novels. "There's too much stuff on the pages and it is confusing about where to find the story and what to look at first." So, I began to review Newbery Award winning books that had a theme and a main character that might engage Maya. I researched reviews and checked out many books from the library before deciding on any. In addition, I asked her English teacher for some recommendations. I investigated those, too, but found the titles tended to be about 40 years old or had a theme that was not likely to engage Maya, so I dismissed them. She gave one piece of advice I agreed with, "find a genre" that Maya would like. I, too, had found that if a "reluctant reader" enjoyed a character, an author's style, or genre, they would often be willing to continue to read more books in the series or genre. Familiarity with the author's format, setting, or main character(s) lessened the cognitive load compared to reading an unfamiliar book. After previewing many books, I selected *Hello, Universe* by Erin Entrada Kelly, *When You Trap a Tiger* by Tae Keller, and *The Baker's Secret* by Stephen P. Kiernan.

*Hello, Universe* won the 2018 Newbery Award and features awkward middle schoolers and shifts between the character's perspectives of events, which would be sufficiently challenging for Maya. The main character, Kaori Tanaka is a self-proclaimed psychic who uses crystals and consults the zodiac. I believed Kaori's quirky nature would appeal to Maya.

*When You Trap a Tiger* won the 2021 Newbery Award, as well as the Asian/Pacific American Award for Children's Literature. It features Korean folklore about a magical tiger that only Lily, the main character, can see. I believed Maya would respond to the folklore aspect and enjoy following Lily's quest to save her grandmother by striking a dangerous bargain with the tiger, even though Lily's grandmother had warned her, "Never trust a tiger."

I selected *The Baker's Secret* as it was from a critically acclaimed author and a book of historical fiction would be a unique challenge. The main character, Emmanuelle, quietly displays courage, determination, optimism, and resilience in her tiny Normandy village on the eve of D-Day. I believed Emmanuelle's strength of character and her story of resistance would attract Maya. The book features wonderful examples of figurative language, which was an excellent vehicle for teaching these literary concepts. Her mother purchased copies of all three books so that we would each have one. Unfortunately, it took Maya much longer to read each book than I had anticipated, so she did not read *The Baker's Secret* until later.

"Writing and reading are related" is the stark statement made by (National Council of Teachers of English's Executive Committee in the Document., 2016). One cannot write about something not really understood. Adequate reading comprehension is a key aspect of clarity in one's writing. "Research has shown that when students receive writing instruction, their reading fluency and comprehension improve.... Without strategies for reading course material and opportunities to write thoughtfully about it, students have difficulty mastering concepts. These literacy practices are firmly linked with both thinking and learning." I have termed this practice as "cross-training" which links adolescent reading and writing skills.

## Reading – *Hello, Universe*

Chapters 3–6 of this book detailed the types of shorter passages Maya was asked to read and respond to in writing. Now, it was time to have her engage in reading longer texts. Without any competing homework assignments, she was asked to read in sessions and read independently between sessions. Maya was given the choice of which book she would read first. She chose *Hello, Universe*. She explained that she had studied the illustrations on each book cover and then read the description on the backs. "The back cover is like a movie trailer", explained Maya using her cinematic touchpoint. Had I chosen for her, it would have been my choice, too, as it had the shortest chapters. We took turns reading aloud for the first several pages.

"Can I read in my head?" Maya asked.

"Okay", was my response. We both read silently for the next five minutes. She had read four pages in that time, which was close to my pace, so I wondered how well she was comprehending it.

"Maya, why did Virgil get shoved into the wall by the bully, Chet?"

"Huh? I don't know. I guess I was reading too fast to notice that."

I had momentarily forgotten that she had never read a book independently and, for her entire 7th-grade year, her Resource teacher had been giving her the answers to comprehension questions. Maya had no prior experience with comprehending a novel, as she had only listened to assigned audiobooks.

"You are going to use your sticky notes, again. Blue is for words you don't know."

Maya interrupted, "Green is important details and pink is for important ideas. I remember."

"What does *debilitate* mean?"

"I don't know. I will mark it in blue."

"Yes. Can you figure it out from the context?"

"Maybe like . . . weak? Can I look it up?"

"Sure. Then, write the meaning on your "blue sticky."

At the end of the session, I asked her to read the next two chapters on her own, in between sessions and using her "sticky notes"; Maya agreed. In the next session, she had good recall and I asked her to read from her own "sticky notes" and we compared where she had marked and where I had. I explained that different parts might be interesting for different readers, which was fine, but that we ought to have marked the same passages which contained essential details and key ideas. *Hello, Universe* switches in every chapter with the main characters taking turns explaining what is occurring. She had missed that. I asked her to go back and read silently the beginning of the last two chapters and tell me who was narrating the story.

"Oh! I missed that. Virgil was talking and now it is Valencia."

## Making Predictions

As we each read the next chapter silently, Maya exclaimed, "I bet Valencia will go to the psychic to help her with her bad dreams!" I knew she was correct but did not signal that. Instead, I asked her to use a yellow "sticky" to write down her prediction.

At the next session, it was apparent that Maya had read the assigned chapters with good recall of the events.

"You know how *else* you can tell who is telling the story now?" Maya asked me.

"No", was my honest reply.

"Each character has a little symbol and it is always at the top of each new chapter. See, Virgil's is a turtle [his nickname]."

"Wow", I said as I quickly checked the beginning of several chapters. "You are right! Good noticing, Maya!" Again, Maya was keenly aware of visual details.

"Be thinking about how each character is feeling in each new chapter, so we can discuss it."

Maya read three short chapters, on her own, between sessions, and was able to summarize each character's feelings. "So far, it's all happening on Saturday. Is everything going to take place on one day?" she asked. She was absolutely correct; the story takes place on a single day.

"Write that down on a yellow, Maya. That is a really interesting prediction." I told her that it did not actually matter if her predictions are correct. What mattered is that the reader was making them. "Why are making predictions a good idea, Maya?"

"Because it shows you are paying attention to what's happening and thinking", she answered promptly.

## Pacing

The pace of reading the book seemed inordinately slow to me. Although she read two or three chapters at a time, that only amounted to 10–12 pages. I had to remind myself that she had never developed any "reading stamina."

Maya's schedule became very irregular without school. She stayed up late and was not always medicated. "I forgot", was her simple reply. She could not recall the "i" before "e" spelling rule and she turned two pages at once and did not notice that the next page made no sense. I noted this and reminded Maya about the importance of taking her medication. At the next session, Maya was medicated, demonstrated logical thinking, was reading for meaning, and was able to orally summarize the last chapters, including each character's feelings.

"If I were writing this book, I would make Sacred (a stray dog) Valencia's pet and train him as a medical dog"; Valencia is deaf.

When discussing which of the characters she might wish to write about, Maya said, "Probably Kaori", the main character.

"Why?"

"Because she reminds me of myself! She believes in crystals, the zodiac, and . . . she's punctual!"

## Mark and Defend

At times, Maya was still struggling with summarizing the chapter she had just read. However, she could always refer to her "sticky notes" and "stringing them together" which helped her summarize. In order to move past merely selecting essential information, I introduced a new technique that I had created for college students who were struggling with reading comprehension. I had titled it "Mark and Defend" (Marshall, 2014. Research-Based Comprehension Strategies for Writers: Reading to Write). One uses a "sticky note" to mark a key detail or an idea, as Maya was doing. With the college students, I limited the number of notes to no more than four or five per chapter of a novel, to help establish saliency. Students would tell me they initially marked a passage but later realized it was not as critical as something else. "You can't always know what's important until you have read the whole chapter", was one insightful comment. In addition, one needed to be able to explain *why* you had marked that place in the text. She was intrigued by this new "challenge" and was trying to convince me *why* her citations were better than mine.

Maya, like some other students, most naturally gravitated to details, but could not readily summon them into "the big picture." I asked her to "gather up" her sticky notes into a "big idea." I held my hands widespread, slowly bringing them together until my fingertips touched, to demonstrate this concept. Again, I chose my language purposefully, as Maya was fully aware that summarizing was still difficult for her. Gradually, she became better at gathering up details and creating the "big idea", which was a good summary. Although creating a summary was effortful, she continued to make logical predictions. "Do you think they will use the jump rope to get Virgil out of the well?" (Kaori's little sister carries a jump rope everywhere and they *do* use it to rescue Virgil from the well.)

Maya finished the book and was able to write answers to open-ended questions about it. "Maya, why do you think the book is titled, "*Hello Universe?*" She thought for a while considering the question.

"Well, at the end of Chapter 28, Virgil's grandmother says that the universe is the always sending out messages," Maya said. She went on to explain, "I think some people don't get them because they don't believe in them. Everyone but Chet seems open to receiving them. Virgil is just beginning to believe in that while he is stuck down in the well. Kaori is a natural!"

"Can you write that down?" I asked.

She had read the first book since 3rd grade with good understanding. How would she rate this book, on a scale of 1–10 with Charlotte Doyle being a 1?

"A 7.5", Maya stated; however, she added she *would* recommend it to her friends. Her first draft description of Kaori's character study is as follows:

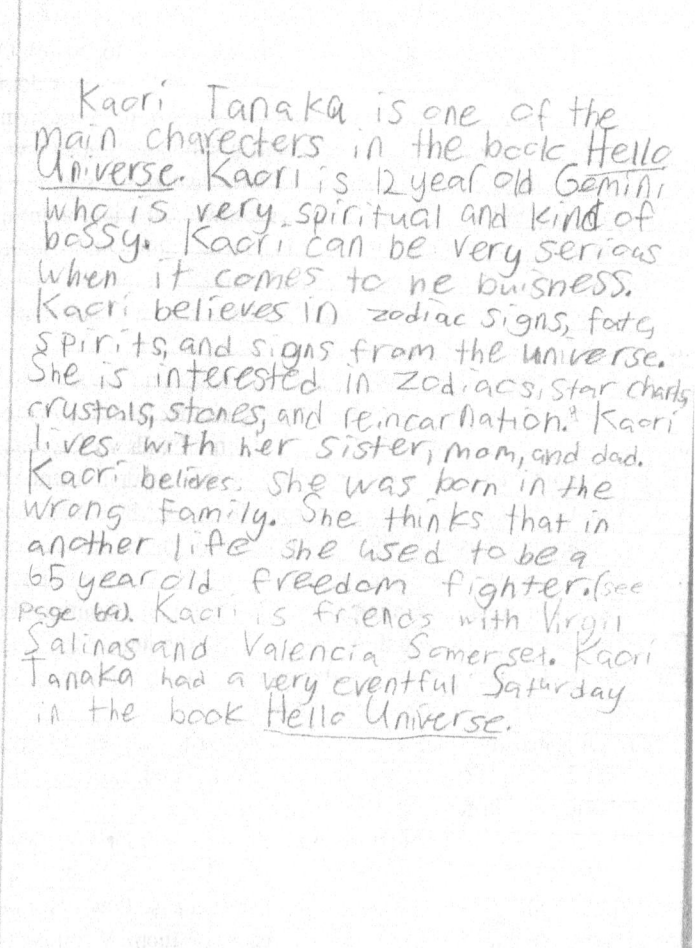

*Figure 7.1* Kaori – Character Study

## Reading – *When You Trap a Tiger*

Next, she chose to read *When You Trap a Tiger*, after studying the cover and description on the back cover. "What's with the jar with stars coming out of it? Is this going to be like a genie in a bottle story?"

"Now, that's interesting, Maya. Write that down on a yellow stickie, as your first prediction."

"Am I right?" she asked.

"You'll see", was my enigmatic answer.

Maya was reading with good understanding but complained about some of the chapters being "soooo long." The last chapter she had read was 9 ½ pages in length. I began asking that she read two chapters independently between sessions. Her notes were accurate and she could defend *why* she had marked a passage, employing the "Mark and Defend" technique. In creating her written summary of chapters read, sometimes punctuation was missing. Maya was concentrating on writing her summary, so her focus was diffused. The cognitive load of integrating all these new writing skills was taxing. An ET must be aware of the student's attentional capacity, at any given time, and the demands of integrating relatively new skills.

"Why do I have to keep correcting things?"

"I think you know why."

"I have to do it until it becomes a habit."


## Her Reading Expands

Maya was reading the book with interest now and making frequent predictions. It surprised me how often they were correct, although I did not reveal that; instead, I asked that she write them down. "I have a whole page of them! I'm keeping them inside the front cover of my book."

Then, she surprised me by reading two more chapters, over a weekend, without being asked to do so. Was she becoming a reader? Maya's mother texted me. She wrote, "You won't believe this. We are in the mall. Maya asked to go into the bookstore. She has selected some books for me to buy. She wants to read them!"

However, Maya noticed her mother texting. She became nearly hysterical when she learned her mother had texted me. "Why are you so upset, Maya? I thought Ms. Marion would be pleased to know you chose some books to read on your own."

"No!" Maya wailed. "She'll make me take notes!"

So, in our next session, I causally asked to see the books she had selected. Maya pouted, "I don't want to show you."

"Why not?" I asked. She repeated what she had told her mother.

"Ah, I get that- except there are two kinds of books, Maya. Some you read just for enjoyment (no notes needed) and there are others, like in school, you take notes on to be able to remember or quote from them," I said.

"Wait. Wait. I can **just** read them? Okay!" she exclaimed happily as she ran across her room to get a stack of books and then, held each up to the camera to explain why each appealed to her. At the end of the session, Maya agreed to read two more chapters independently before our sessions. I was floored when she added, "And I could write a summary from my notes."

About a week later, her father texted me a picture of Maya sitting on the floor of a department store they frequented. Apparently, he had searched everywhere in the toy department where she usually shopped. He could not find her until he came upon her in the book section – with a large stack of books next to her. She was reading.

Maya finished reading *When You Trap a Tiger* and offered to create a "movie trailer" to summarize the book. I thought it was a perfect ending since her 8th-grade year was about to start. I agreed and asked her to review her predictions, as another kind of culminating event. She began reading each aloud and discussed whether she had been accurate. She had made 12 predications; 7 of them were wholly correct and she informed me that "two more were kinda correct."

At the end of summer, her mother texted me a picture of Maya reading in the car on their family vacation. It was a book I had casually mentioned that she might enjoy reading sometime.

Maya was excited to go back to school, primarily to be in class with her friends again.

"Want to see how I answered my English teacher's 'introduce yourself' questions?"

"Yes, I do", was my response.

The questions were asked before school resumed. Among others, her teacher asked each student to list their three favorite activities; Maya showed me her answer:

1. read books
2. listen to music
3. watch movies

"Are you just saying you like to read to impress her?" I asked.

"No. It really *is* my favorite thing to do", Maya replied firmly, as if she had been enjoying reading for years.

Nancy Patterson, in a *Voices from the Middle* article (Patterson, N., 2012) raises the point, "If the whole idea behind English language arts classes is to foster a love of reading and a thirst for human experience and ideas represented through text, then we have to think critically about not only the kinds of reading our students do, but also the kinds of writing they do."

## IEP Meeting to Begin 8th Grade

Since the new school year was beginning, the new resource specialist sent over a date for an IEP to "establish her baseline" and set annual goals. Both sides agreed to meet without the lawyers. Maya's parents and I met virtually to plan what points to stress. Her mother had written a list of accommodations she planned to present.

"Most of these are not really accommodations", I said. "They seem to be a list of teaching do's and don'ts."

"Well, I feel like that is what they need to hear", she answered.

I suggested being ready to weave her points into our comments but not insist that they be deemed accommodations. She agreed reluctantly. The district emailed the IEP draft document and new goals. Everything appeared reasonable. However, one day before the scheduled IEP meeting, a new IEP was emailed to Maya's parents. Her mother texted me frantically, "Urgent! Help! I just sent you an email. Please read the new IEP – am I reading it correctly?"

Unfortunately, the latest IEP document now stated that Maya was being exited from special education – again!

"Yes, you are reading the latest IEP correctly."

"Didn't we fight this all of last year?" her mother sobbed into the phone.

"Don't panic. You have a court order – remember? Contact your lawyer immediately."

## Summary

This Educational Therapist's and the family's roles in preparing for the trial to restore Maya's special education services and her IEP were described. Startling evidence of Maya's teachers' editing "supports" were detailed. Maya's family won their legal case, but further challenges regarding establishing the benchmarks for Maya's goals appeared. Her parents employed the same neuropsychologist to reassess her. Significant gains in Maya's skills were documented. Over the summer, Maya began reading novels (for the first time) and began to enjoy reading. A surprising and dramatic last-minute challenge to Maya's status ends this chapter.

## References

National Council of Teachers of English's Executive Committee in the Document. (2016). *Professional Knowledge for the Teaching of Writing.* https://ncte.org/statement/teaching-writing

Parental Rights to Records. www.fetaweb.com/04/ferpa.rooker.ltr.protocols.htm and www.wrightslaw.com/law/caselaw/05/2005.CA.dist.court.newport-mesa.test.protocols.pdf

Patterson, N. (2012). *Voices from the middle.* https://library.ncte.org/journals/VM/issues/v12-3/4702

# 8 The Case of Maya
## Summary

Case study research is a qualitative approach in which the investigator explores a real situation, over time, using detailed and in-depth data collection involving multiple sources of information. Yin, (Yin, R. K. *(2018)*. *Case Study Research and Applications: Design and Methods (6th ed.)*. *SAGE Publications)* who is often cited as an expert on case study methodology, states that this method is especially appropriate for determining the "how and why" of phenomena and contributes to understanding these in a holistic real-life context. Others agree that it is particularly well-suited to explaining the outcomes in an individual case and can play an important role in advancing a field's knowledge base.

The case study methodology requires much of the investigator since one must act as both the educational therapist and researcher. As such, this methodology is prone to bias, as the researcher's own subjective feelings may influence the stated results. The researcher may skew the results toward confirming preconceived notions since the researcher decides what evidence to collect and include. Fortunately, in the case of Maya, there is evidence of her growth and progress from a variety of sources: archival records, direct observations, discourse with Maya, informal protocols, and the physical evidence of her writing samples. In addition, the results were documented by the neuropsychologist's assessment and report, an unbiased participant outside of the case.

Further, this researcher did not originally intend to write a case study, so she did not have "preconceived notions" about the outcomes. Rather, she wished to answer the questions raised in Chapter 1. Could wholly virtual educational therapy be efficacious for Maya? Would Maya be a willing partner able to engage in the online format? Could she sustain her attention long enough to benefit from each session? Would the educational therapist be able to sufficiently observe and monitor Maya's internal and emotional states through a computer screen? The answer to each of these was positive so, fortunately, the outcomes far exceeded my expectations.

This researcher is keenly aware and freely acknowledges that few families would have the acumen or financial resources to pursue an IEE, hire a lawyer and an educational therapist to challenge the district's special education decision. The researcher had reduced her work to a very limited caseload which she termed a "micro-practice." That, coupled with being very wary of working *wholly* virtually, the researcher had thought not to take on any new clients. But, as COVID-19 wore on, she thought she might begin with a new student. If her practice had been large, this researcher may not have had the time to create so much "customized" curriculum for Maya. However, please note that the researcher has always utilized the student's interests and affinities to create or choose content. This would have been true whether conducting face-to-face or virtual educational therapy.

Formal reports from allied professionals are often extremely useful and can be affirming. Formal assessment is a "snapshot" of the student, contextualized by the examiner's training and years of experience assessing and observing those who are struggling as learners. However, one should not prioritize assessment results over one's own experience with the student. In fact, ongoing observations and dialogue with the student may provide the most valuable insights. Fortunately, the researcher had already formed a positive partnership with Maya before reading the neuropsychological report. The educational therapist ascertained that, when medicated for ADHD, Maya was a very different and capable learner. In the course of this case study, both Maya and her parents came to appreciate that.

It was very beneficial that the educational therapist had years of experience conducting IEP meetings. Further, the researcher's advocacy skills contributed to the positive outcome. It was also beneficial that Maya knew herself very well. For example, upon reflection, her responses to the Levine interview and executive functioning questions were all accurate. She had many strengths that were masked, underutilized, or simply not valued by Maya, her teachers, or her parents. Maya demonstrated keen logical reasoning skills, analytical questioning, was always punctual, consistently sequenced her writing logically, and enjoyed "thinking games" such as Sudoku. She also demonstrated intellectual curiosity and became a more self-directed learner. In other words, she had many talents that could be applied to school that were "not typical" of a student with significant ADHD. At times, the researcher felt like she had three missions: 1) to help Maya believe in herself as a learner; 2) to assist her teachers in supporting her appropriately; and 3) to enable her parents to see her in a new, more talented light, with the clear potential that she could and *should* go to college. For example, the neuropsychologist told the researcher (in a private communication) that after re-establishing her special education eligibility, Maya's parents would need to investigate private schools, as she would never be able to "make it" in a public high school. At the beginning of the case study, it appeared that everyone had low expectations for Maya succeeding in school – including Maya.

It is believed that a key factor in Maya's success was that, since she had declared the COVID-19 online school year to be a "total waste", it freed her to work more cooperatively and in a more engaged manner with the researcher. She was less distracted by school demands, homework, and her friends. Maya keenly missed having contact with her friends, so it is possible that she transferred some of that "need to connect" to the researcher. Although the researcher never met Maya, she was a willing partner and her candor and lack of guile assisted our work enormously.

Maya was missing many of the fundamentals for writing well. Although she had a diagnosis of dysgraphia, it only affected her letter formation, not the amount she could write at any time. Maya struggled with activating and sustaining attention during the writing process, knowing writing conventions, and applying them. She had not yet learned that writing is written *language*. For many students (especially those with ADHD), the multifaceted demands of writing and the executive functions required are overwhelming. It appeared that Maya had not had the coordinated and well-sequenced explicit instruction necessary to develop her writing skills. When coupled with her school's lack of expectations for her and the lack of feedback about her writing, Maya's skills languished. Educational Therapy addressed this with a careful examination of the skills she had acquired, what was missing, and what was confused.

Although her vocabulary initially appeared limited, she did not have an expressive language disorder. Maya had not read a book since the end of the 3rd grade. Perhaps, she had not acquired the vocabulary of her peers who read regularly. Also, many students who have a written language disorder simplify the vocabulary they use in their writing. This was not the case for Maya who spelled well, in isolation, and used some sophisticated word choices by spelling phonetically. Importantly, as Maya's writing skills became better integrated, her specific written word choices also improved. The researcher theorizes that she had an adequate vocabulary but that it was latent. She could not access it while struggling with the cognitive load of *how* to write using proper writing mechanics. Until the mechanics of written language became more automatic, her vocabulary was masked.

By the end of this case study, Maya became an avid reader who very often made correct predictions. Making predictions was an important way for her to focus when reading a novel, as it is a technique that greatly enhances the student's reading comprehension. Reading and writing are closely related. There is no need to separate these skills, especially for the adolescent. Research has shown that writing about what has been read ("cross-training") benefits development of both skills. As Maya read more, her writing improved as well and she no longer used the "little girl voice", which the researcher had deemed a signal of learned helplessness or asking to be "rescued."

Maya had difficulty creating the "whole" out of "the parts." Learning that is fractured into discrete pieces does not hold one's attention as well, nor is it retained easily. Her difficulty with understanding "the big idea" and creating a summary remained challenging. Maya's struggle to perceive the gestalt became even more evident when she read books. However, as Maya read more chapters and, when shown how to take notes, determine saliency, and "gather up" key information, her ability to grasp the main idea was much improved by the end of the study.

Stake (1995) claimed that much may be learned from a case study and that "readers can learn vicariously" through a case study and "the researcher's narrative descriptions." Applying neuropsychological principles, such as establishing well-defined and specific learning goals, allowed Maya to activate prior learning. Learning goals were created for each session, coupled with visual cues, and encouraged deeper and more lasting learning. When the educational therapist forgot to employ these neuropsychological principles, Maya's learning floundered temporarily.

Many of Maya's confusions regarding punctuation resulted from a lack of clear demarcation in new learning and her attempts to create meaning for something not understood. Demarcation may not occur when two similar sounding or related concepts are taught too close together and become co-mingled (e.g., plurals and possessives). The frank and ongoing process-oriented dialogue between Maya and the researcher allowed these misunderstandings to emerge and these concepts were retaught. At the end of the study, Maya had "sparked" with more self-directed learning and improved her metacognition. For example,

"Do you need a break?"

"No, I'm good. I am writing."

Lastly, this book adds to the very limited literature on the efficacy of providing Educational Therapy services virtually. Most educational therapists began practicing virtual educational therapy out of necessity and by thinking, "This is better than nothing" for their clients. The researcher learned that **all** of the supports provided in face-to-face educational therapy were **essential** for providing effective ET virtually. New requirements were a basic comfort level and proficiency with technology and a selection of a secure delivery platform. What was not new and still critical were: 1) establishing a partnership between client and educational therapist; 2) monitoring the client's level of attention; 3) monitoring the length of time of sustained attention; 4) a careful sequencing and structuring of curricula delivered incrementally; 5) creation of ongoing and respectful dialogue between the client and clinician; 6) careful observation of the client's emotional state – especially if highly variable; and 7) establishing clear learning goals for each session. Also, in this instance, being an advocate for the child with her parents and school was an important role. Lastly, the most critical aspect of effective virtual educational therapy was establishing a consistently high degree of client **engagement.**

Using research-based techniques to improve student engagement and attention was critical to Maya's success. Following Maya's interests and expanding on them created a pathway to in-depth learning. Her writing skills rose from the 7th percentile rank to the 61st percentile rank, **even though unmedicated** when reassessed. The researcher concludes that Maya had actually deeply learned these requisite skills. Readers are challenged to consider applying these, as well as the other specific educational therapy techniques described, to their own work, especially when working online. In addition, this case study adds to the literature and may well serve as a model for others wanting to learn about educational therapy and for those preparing to write a case study.

## Summary

Maya advanced her writing skills to the 61st percentile rank for her age, even when unmedicated as assessed by the same neuropsychologist one year later. Applying research-based techniques to improve her engagement and attention combined well with specific educational therapy strategies. Maya's written expression skills advanced significantly and subsequently her interest in reading flourished.

## References

Stake, R. E. (1995). *The art of case study research.* SAGE Publications.

Yin, R. K. (2013). *Case study research and applications: Design and methods* (6th ed.). SAGE Publications.

# Index

accommodations 30, 59, 75
advocate 4, 17, 28, 81
arbitration 29, 30, 37, 60
attention-deficit/hyperactivity disorder (ADHD) 1, 2, 4, 5, 8, 19, 25, 46, 66, 78–79

Barnett, Mac 42, 44
Behavior Assessment System for Children–3 5
Behavior Rating Inventory of Executive Function – 2nd Edition 5, 66
Bell, Nanci 25

California Office of Administrative Hearings 30
case study methodology xi, xii, 77
Children and Adolescent Memory Profile 5, 66
Children's Memory Scale 5
cognitive load 14, 73, 79
Common Core Standards for English Language Arts 28, 31, 37

demarcation 18, 25, 80
dysgraphia 1, 36, 64, 79

EBSCO xi, xii
engagement 6, 12, 20, 21, 36, 81
executive functioning skills 6, 8, 59, 65–66, 78

FERPA 63, 76
Flexible Spending Account (FSA) 44

Four Square graphic organizer method 12–15, 19–21, 28, 35, 53

Grammarly 29, 31
Gray Oral Reading Test – V 5
Greek gods and goddesses 9, 45, 47

*Hello, Universe* 67–69, 71

ideation 3, 8
Independent Educational Evaluation (IEE) 3, 4, 17, 78

Kaufman Test of Educational Achievement–3 5

learning goals 25, 80, 81
learning purpose 25, 33
local educational agencies (LEAs) 64

mad libs 18, 50, 56
margin notes 53
mark and defend 71, 73
metacognition 66, 80

Newbery Award 67–68

other health impaired 8

persuasive essay 52
process approach 9, 20
process-oriented dialogue 79–80
projective drawings 5

ReadWorks 26, 31, 33, 45
release of information 40
Rey-Osterrieth Complex Figure 5, 7

saliency 6, 54–56, 71, 80
self-directed learning 19, 51, 56, 80
Sitton, Rebecca 15, 22
Specific Learning Disability (SLD) 1, 5, 8
stay put order 4, 28

Test of Variables of Attention (TOVA) 6
Test of Written Language-4 (TOWL-4) 5, 32, 64–65
tomtar/tomte 38, 41–44
transference 52, 56, 79

Visualizing and Verbalizing® Language 25
*Voices from the Middle* 74, 76

Wechsler Individual Achievement Test® Third Edition (WIAT-3) 37, 61–65
Wechsler Individual Achievement Test® Fourth Edition (WIAT-4) 32, 60, 63
Wechsler Intelligence Scale for Children – V (WISC-V) 5
*When You Trap a Tiger* 67–68, 73–74
Woodcock-Johnson IV Tests of Achievement (WJ IV ACH) 17, 32

For Product Safety Concerns and Information please contact our EU
representative GPSR@taylorandfrancis.com
Taylor & Francis Verlag GmbH, Kaufingerstraße 24, 80331 München, Germany

www.ingramcontent.com/pod-product-compliance
Lightning Source LLC
Chambersburg PA
CBHW070601170426
43201CB00012B/1900